Hiking

NEW
HOLLAND

Hiking

Jacques Marais

First published in 2002
This edition published in 2009 by
New Holland Publishers
London • Cape Town • Sydney • Auckland
www.newhollandpublishers.com

Garfield House, 86–88 Edgware
Road, London W2 2EA
United Kingdom

80 McKenzie Street
Cape Town 8001
South Africa

Unit 1, 66 Gibbes Street
Chatswood, NSW 2067
Australia

218 Lake Road
Northcote, Auckland
New Zealand

ISBN 978 1 84773 342 9

Publishing manager: Claudia dos Santos
Managing editor: Simon Pooley
Managing art editor: Richard MacArthur
Commissioning editor: Karyn Richards
Editor: Gill Gordon
Designer: Christelle Marais
Illustrator: Steven Felmore
Picture researcher: Bronwyn Allies
Proofreader: Tinkie Arnold
Production: Myrna Collins
Consultant: Steve Razzetti

Reproduction by Hirt & Carter (Pty) Ltd, Cape Town
Printed and bound in Singapore by Craft Print (Pte) Ltd

2 4 6 8 10 9 7 5 3

Disclaimer
Although the author and publishers
have made every effort to ensure that
the information contained in this book
was accurate at the time of going to
press, they accept no responsibility for
any accident, loss or inconvenience
that is sustained by any person using
this book or the advice given in it.

Author's acknowledgements

Making a book is a huge process that evolves over time and involves many role players, some of whom don't even realize the part they have played. I owe a huge debt to my parents, who gave me the confidence to walk tall, and to my wife Cathy, who has tramped many miles with me through rain and shine, sharing a love of nature and the great outdoors. Without them, I may never have begun the journey.

I would also like to thank the production team at New Holland; the photographers, illustrator, designer and especially my editor, Gill Gordon, who assisted in making this publication possible.

A final word must, however, go to the many canine companions who have kept me company since my first faltering steps and who, I hope, will continue to walk with me, in body and spirit, for decades to come.

Contents

The culture of walking

All that is gold does not glitter, not all those who wander are lost.
J.R.R. Tolkien ~ The Lord of the Rings

Our ability to walk upright is thought to date back to the Early Stone Age, a period more than one and a half million years ago. It was then that our ancestors stood upright and gingerly took their first steps. These small steps would prove to be a proverbial giant leap, allowing humankind to fast-track its development along evolution's long and winding road. Walking on two legs allowed our forebears to develop and use sophisticated tools, quickly turning them into a dominant hunter-gatherer society.

So it was that mankind became walkers, striding proudly upright across the vast plains of ancient continents. As hunter-gatherers, they walked out of a necessity to support their nomadic lifestyle rather than for pleasure, searching the wilderness for food and shelter. Slowly this natural landscape changed as evolution marched on, with first agriculture and then industrialization taking its toll. Vast cities of concrete and steel mushroomed throughout the developed world, replacing trees, rivers, grasslands and forests with tarmac roads and soaring skyscrapers. Green belts and parklands all but disappeared in some places and soon many city dwellers found themselves captives of an unnatural environment of their own making.

Which brings us to where we are now at the beginning of the 21st century and, some would say, with civilization at its technological peak. Many of us find ourselves in a position where we have more income, resources and free time at our disposal than any previous generation. And, in order to escape the pressure and stress of our urban environment, we buy ourselves some time in the great outdoors, because it is here that we are able to rediscover the instinctive simplicity that came so easily to our cavemen ancestors. And what better way to get in touch with our earthy side than by exploring the many natural splendours of our planet on foot?

Stepping out

In essence, walking is about undertaking small journeys of discovery. It might not be exploration on the grand scale of a Marco Polo discovering far-flung corners of the globe, but it still captures the sensation of travelling into the (ever so slightly) unknown. You might be on a well-trodden track, a route that you have walked many times before, but such is the beauty of nature that it will show you a new face every time.

A glimpse of scarlet in the undergrowth might uncover a previously unnoticed flower, or a flash of feathery blue will reveal a kingfisher flitting along a stream bed. Over the years, a hiking route will become like an old friend, ageing with you and mellowing as you get to know it better. Seasons will herald joyful changes along a regular trail, dressing it in splashes of colour in spring, or shades of green in summer, while winter will bring with it the return of stark and simple lines. Over time, trees will shake off their spindly adolescence, spreading gnarly branches in greeting when you again encounter them after a decade or two. It does not matter how many times you travel a certain way — every walk will bring with it new discoveries, allowing you to explore to your heart's content.

On good terms

Over the generations, as we tramped along our bridle-ways, country lanes and mountain paths, some walkers donned rucksacks, dressed in technical clothing and took to using specially designed equipment. Walking

WONDERING WHAT LIES OVER THE HORIZON OR AROUND THE NEXT BEND KEEPS MANY HIKERS GOING. CHALK CLIFFS, DORSET, ENGLAND.

YOU CAN HIKE, AND ENJOY IT, IN ALL CLIMATES AND WEATHER CONDITIONS. WALKING THROUGH SNOWY WOODS CAN CREATE A SENSE OF BEING THE ONLY PERSON EVER TO HAVE PASSED THAT WAY, AN EXPERIENCE THAT URBAN DWELLERS MAY FIND QUITE EXHILARATING.

was no longer just a stroll in the wilds, and a host of new terms and expressions was born. Nowadays, people go hiking, trailing and backpacking all over the world. High on ridged peaks, mountaineers traverse; in canyons or gorges, individuals dabble in canyoneering or kloofing; clamber on all fours up a steep scree slope and you are elevated into the realm of scrambling; follow a route hugging the coastline and you'll be pleased to know that you are coasteering. Many related terms exist and, although it is impossible to cover all of them in this book, a later chapter will look at a selection of specialized walking disciplines.

Before we boot up though, it is useful to define two universally accepted terms associated with walking: hiking and backpacking. Although the word back-packing was originally coined to describe the process of walking in the outdoors with a pack on your back, and is a term widely used in the USA, in other parts of the world backpacking is usually associated with budget travel, and hiking has replaced it as the term used to describe a walk in nature, along a well-marked, defined pathway or route. Therefore, depending on which country you are in, you will find both hikers and backpackers walking along a trail in a conservancy or a state forest, across a public common, or in a national park, following a clearly signposted route, possibly with the assistance of a map, a trail-guide, or both.

Hikes can be either single-day or short routes, or long trails that require a number of days, even weeks, to complete. Many multi-day hikes traverse wilderness areas without the aid of marked trails, with hikers having to move from Point A to Point B, possibly along a compass bearing, or with the aid of map coordinates, and usually encountering a wide variety of terrain. These expeditionary, or wilderness, hikes are usually more rigorous than hiking along marked trails and require detailed planning and preparation, as well as a higher level of experience from participants. They are frequently in remote locations, and may involve a group of people with a range of specialist skills.

So far, so good, but the small matter of terminology does not quite end here either. Travel beyond the borders of your home country and you'll find people talking a different walk. In New Zealand, the outdoor tribe go tramping; and Australians venture into the outback for a bush walk. A ramble across the moors might be the norm in England, but many South Africans prefer trailing, while Americans and Canadians stick to either bushwhacking or backpacking.

Venture beyond the comfortable cocoon of the first world and you will encounter a further culture shift, discovering that most people in developing countries rarely walk for pleasure. To them, walking is often an economic reality, but this does not mean that they take no pleasure from it. On the contrary, walking is often an integral part of courtship rituals and other traditional rites, allowing individuals or groups time to get to know each other.

The next step

A final observation: venturing into the great outdoors for a walk is often not about reaching a destination. For most of us, a walk is about the enjoyment of a journey on foot between two points, allowing us to take pleasure from a heady blend of fresh air, scenic views and simple exercise. Sweeping panoramas, the emerald glow of a deep forest at noon, or the invigorating scent of a mountainside alive with heather are sure to put a spring in your step.

Soon you will feel the blood coursing through your body as you leave the daily grind behind and relish the freedom of the great outdoors. Along the way, take time out to lie beneath a spreading canopy of ancient trees, or admire the majesty of the mountains, soaking up the enchantment of nature. As our planet revolves under its wide blue sky, bask in the beauty of your surroundings. After all, unlike our cavemen ancestors, you are walking because you choose to, not because you have to.

STOPPING TO ENJOY NATURAL BEAUTY ALONG THE WAY EMPHASIZES ONE OF THE KEY LESSONS OF HIKING; THAT WHEN YOU WALK FOR PLEASURE, THE JOURNEY IS MORE IMPORTANT THAN THE DESTINATION.

Planning and preparation

different people get into hiking for different reasons. Some do it to get fit, others to de-stress, some to meet new people (or maybe spend more time with friends and family), while many walk to escape the constant rush of the rat race. Whatever your personal reasons for wanting to become a wanderer, there are important decisions you will need to make before entering into a committed relationship with the outdoors. These decisions will be easier if you are clear as to why you want to walk.

Evaluating your ability

Let us assume, for the moment, that you are a babe in the woods and have never ventured further into the wild than beyond your slightly overgrown back garden. But all of that is about to change; you have bought a rucksack and boots and are ready to hit the trail. The time for evaluation is now – where you are in your life, how old you are, your level of physical fitness, what your social circumstances are, how big your budget is and the amount of free time you have available – as it is within this context that you need to plan your most effective entry into Planet Outdoors.

A hiking state of mind

Your mental and physical capabilities should be your foremost consideration. To really enjoy hiking, you need to enter into an outdoor mind-set. Nature is often unpredictable and you need to accept this from the word go, preparing yourself to deal with uncertainty and, therefore, with the occasional surprise. This uncertainty will almost certainly progress beyond mere mental discomfort to test your limits on the physical side as well. Fatigue, perspiration, insect bites, scratches, hypothermia, abrasions, twisted ankles, leeches and midges are all part and parcel of the hiking experience and you need to prepare both your mind and body to handle these situations.

One way to do this is to think of possible scenarios which you might have to face and try to imagine how you would cope. A simple scenario (which almost all hikers have to deal with at some stage) is getting lost on a trail late in the afternoon with a storm brewing. You all get wet, it gets dark, you are unable to locate a suitable camp site and the mood gets ugly. This can happen to anyone, even the most experienced of hikers, and it could mean that you end up spending a very cold and rainy night out in the wild. Consider how you might have avoided this situation in the first place and also how you would react if it did occur.

above BEFORE YOU LEAVE, IT'S IMPORTANT TO EVALUATE YOUR ABILITY AND THINK ABOUT THE ROLE THAT TERRAIN WILL PLAY.
opposite PREPARING AND PACKING IS PART OF THE HIKING RITUAL, AND IS CRITICAL TO THE SUCCESS OF ANY HIKE, EVEN A ONE-DAY WALK.

A CERTAIN AGILITY IS NEEDED TO DANCE ACROSS ROCKS WITH THE GRACE OF A GAZELLE, SO DON'T MAKE THE MISTAKE OF ASSUMING THAT YOU DON'T NEED TO BE FIT TO HIKE.

one 5km (3-mile) ramble on the weekend would be a good start. Slowly build this up to a stage where you can comfortably walk 15km (9 miles) in a day, spending in the region of five to seven hours on your feet.

Remember that you will have to do this with a pack on your back, so break in your body by starting off with a light day pack, gradually increasing its weight. Your day pack will rarely weigh more than 8kg (17 lb), but you would be surprised at how much this additional weight can affect your posture and breathing.

Set goals for yourself, but make sure these are realistic and achievable, otherwise disappointment will creep in, spoiling a fun, fresh-air day. Keep in mind that hiking should be first and foremost about enjoyment. Of course it will sometimes be necessary to push the boundaries a bit, but a walk should never become a grind.

Joining a walking club

Some people are not into clubs or associations, while others appreciate the motivation and company offered by a group of walkers. (In some countries, it is necessary to evaluate the crime situation and it might therefore be wise to walk with a group in areas where security is risky).

Check the sport section in your local community newspaper for hiking notices, as there might be an informal group of ramblers active near you. Community bulletin boards, suburban information centres, bird-watching groups, a mountain club or a local outdoor retail store might also be able to put you in touch with hiking clubs in your area.

The benefits of joining a club are obvious — you will be part of a social group of like-minded individuals and

Getting physical

Physical ability varies from person to person and you must prepare your body for what lies ahead. Depending on the level of hike you are planning and your personal fitness, it may be necessary to do muscle and aerobic training in order to get into shape. The easiest way to achieve this is with the help of a walking programme.

If you've never been on a hiking trail before, start off slowly; two walks of 3km (1.8 miles) a week, plus the chances are good that, within such a structured organization, there will be individuals with various levels of hiking experience. As a beginner therefore, you will not need to feel intimidated, and there may be many members willing to share their expertise. Most clubs and associations arrange regular day hikes and weekend excursions, allowing you to build up experience in a safe and informative environment.

Trail etiquette (which varies from region to region and country to country), will also come more easily through contact with other hikers and by observing their actions during an excursion. On the down side, you may be required to pay membership fees, commit to prescribed responsibilities within the organization and lose out on the option of being able to choose your own route, but this is a small price to pay.

Furthermore, being a member of a hiking club will expose you to the concept of group dynamics. Moving at the pace of the slowest walker, for example, will teach you patience (or motivate you to get fitter, if you are keeping the group back). You will also learn about the various responsibility areas within a hiking party. Who will research the trail or arrange permits, whether specialized equipment is required, and who will be responsible for the first-aid kit are just a few of the many tasks that may be distributed within the group.

Group dynamics also extend to interpersonal relationships, so make sure that friends or family members invited on hikes have similar expectations to your own. Children may be especially tricky, and it will be necessary to motivate them during their initial walks and reward them for completing what might seem like an arduous route march. Appointing a hike leader works well in some situations and it will be partly his or her responsibility to lift spirits when everyone is feeling footsore and tired.

HIKING AS PART OF A CLUB OR GROUP HAS MANY SOCIAL BENEFITS, AS WELL AS PROVIDING ACCESS TO EXPERIENCED AND KNOWLEDGEABLE HIKERS. IT IS A GOOD IDEA TO JOIN A HIKING CLUB WHEN YOU BEGIN WALKING, SO THAT YOU CAN GAIN CONFIDENCE TO GO IT ALONE.

Choosing your first trail

If you have gone the route of joining a club, many of the decisions you need to make will be group decisions and some discussion will be required to reach consensus. Start comfortably, from the point of view of both the physical challenge and the relevant logistics. A day hike within the immediate vicinity of your home town or city is a good choice. Make sure you have enough time to reach your destination, complete your hike and return home with some daylight hours to spare in case anything does go wrong.

Getting the research right

The so-called 'anatomy of an area', including its physical landscape, weather patterns and fauna and flora will to some extent determine the conditions you may encounter along your route.

General guidelines are that the further you move away from the equator, the colder it will be and the less it will rain; the higher your altitude above sea level, the lower the temperature; and seasonal cycles bring rain, snow or heat – but never take this for granted, as unpredictable weather conditions often result from air rising over high mountain ranges or through the heating and cooling effects of coastal sea currents.

In order to avoid nasty surprises on those initial day hikes, it's better to stick to areas you know reasonably well. And when you do start travelling further afield (as you will hopefully do once you've read this book), ascertain whether you might envounter cyclones, tornadoes, floods or other dangerous weather phenomena.

Regardless of whether you are hiking close to home or in a more distant location, the more you are able to find out about your intended trail, the better. An altitude and aspect ratio diagram (showing climbs and descents along the route) will give you an idea of the topography, allowing you to approximate an average speed of advance (a ratio between the distance covered and the time elapsed).

Trail guides are an excellent way to research a route, but make sure the publication is up to date and approved, as routes and physical elements may change a great deal in just a few years.

General information is usually available from organizations or authorities responsible for maintaining and managing specific trails and it is important to check regulations and access requirements with them. For example, do you need a permit and if so, is one available at the start of the trail or must it be purchased beforehand; are there

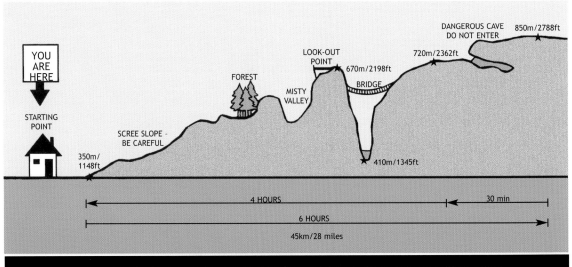

AN ALTITUDE AND ASPECT RATIO DIAGRAM GIVES YOU AN IDEA OF WHAT LIES AHEAD AND WILL HELP YOU TO PLAN YOUR SPEED OF ADVANCE.

THE NUMBER OF HIKERS PERMITTED ON A TRAIL MAY BE LIMITED. TRAIL AUTHORITIES USUALLY HAVE SOUND REASONS FOR THIS, SO OBEY THEM.

limits to the number of hikers allowed on a specific trail; and do you have to book in advance and pay a deposit?

Look for guidebooks or websites on which the trail might be graded according to a difficulty rating, as this will affect your walking speed. Previous hikers might have posted photographs on the Internet, giving you insight into the terrain you will encounter along the way. Large natural obstacles, such as steep rocky slopes, rivers, or canyons with flash flood potential should never be attempted unless you have sufficient experience to deal with the inherent dangers.

Do's and don'ts

■ Do be environmentally aware. Never damage any fauna or flora along the trail. Making fires, walking off the path, picking flowers and disturbing or harming animals are all no-nos.

■ Do be considerate towards other trail users. Do not litter in any way and always ascribe to trail etiquette (this includes avoiding noise pollution such as shouting or loud music).

■ Do protect yourself. In summer, protect against sunburn and hyperthermia (over-heating) by wearing a hat and a lightweight, breathable, long-sleeved shirt and apply sun block regularly. In winter, rain, snow and freezing weather may cause hypothermia (low body temperature), so dress accordingly. Wet clothes (eg cotton T-shirts) speed up body temperature loss, so an outer shell (or raincoat) is imperative to cut down wind chill.

■ Do walk with at least two companions. That way, if an accident or emergency occurs, one person can remain with the injured party while the other goes for help.

■ Do leave a trail itinerary and an estimated time of return with somebody who will take appropriate action if something does go wrong.

■ Do not assume that drinking water will be available along the trail. Always carry an emergency supply of at least 1 litre (2 pints) of water for every two hours of walking.

■ Straying off the designated trail causes erosion, as does throwing stones or rolling rocks off cliffs, so don't do it!

■ On an unknown trail, never walk without a map. It is easy to get lost in an area you do not know well, even one close to home.

■ Don't try out new shoes on a long hike. Rather, break them in gently around the home and during shorter walks until you are sure they are comfortable and won't cause blisters.

RESPECT THE ENVIRONMENT AND YOUR FELLOW HIKERS BY OBSERVING BASIC TRAIL ETIQUETTE, AS WELL AS ANY SPECIFIC REGULATIONS APPLICABLE TO YOUR ROUTE.

BY STICKING TO THE MARKED TRAIL YOU WILL AVOID TRAMPLING OR OTHERWISE DAMAGING POTENTIALLY DELICATE PLANTS THAT GROW ALONGSIDE THE PATH.

Respecting the environment

If you want to keep on enjoying nature, you've got to make sure you put back what you take out. The limited number of hiking ways and trail systems, ever-increasing hiker densities on popular trails, and ecologically insensitive hikers are taking their toll on many over-utilized routes. It requires a concerted effort from the entire hiking community to ensure that future generations can one day follow in our footsteps.

Even though the philosophy of 'leaving nothing but footprints' may sound like a cliché, it holds as true now, as when the first piece of used toilet paper littered a previously pristine trail. Constant awareness of the consequence of your behaviour on the trail is necessary, so find out about specific rules and etiquette along the route (for example, always close gates behind you on private land). Often, damage is done without an individual actually realizing it, so make it your duty to educate yourself and your companions regarding environmental issues.

Fauna and flora

The golden rule is to stick to the designated trail, no matter how big the temptation to take a short cut or step off the path to get a better view. Trailscapers follow very specific contours and use switchbacks in order to avoid erosion, as water rushing along a footpath can soon turn it into a ravine. In delicate desert habitats, stepping off the trail may damage seedlings germinating just beneath the surface and you will also leave traces of your tracks for years to come.

Be aware of your environment and try to tread in places where your footsteps will do the least damage. Limit your group size, walk in single file, and seek out solid hard-pack or rock when you can, avoiding stepping on regrowth along trail edges. Picking flowers or plants along a route is tantamount to signing your own expulsion order from the hiking community, and do not collect dead wood for fires unless permitted to do so. The decomposition of dead plant matter is imperative in the nutrient and mineral cycle enriching the soil, so stick to the 'no fire' rule wherever it is enforced.

Remember that you will be sharing the trail and its surrounding environment with snakes, spiders, wasps, scorpions, leeches and other loveable little nasties intent on protecting what is their rightful home. Keep your distance where you can and in most cases you will be able to avoid a painful confrontation. In case you do stray into the firing line, make sure you have a well-stocked first-aid kit on hand.

If you encounter wildlife on the trail, stick to looking rather than touching. Handling an immature animal or bird might not seem wrong, but the chances are the mother will discard her offspring because of your human smell, leaving it to die. Even the most innocent animal might pack an unexpected punch, leaving you with bites or scratches that could turn septic. When approaching large animals in wilderness areas, do so with caution, giving them a wide berth if possible.

Joining a volunteer group

Hiking is a long-term commitment and it is imperative to preserve trails for future generations. With urban development constantly encroaching on our green spaces, it might be necessary to throw your weight behind a pressure group, sign a few petitions or join in a demonstration to preserve an unspoiled area.

Other ways of giving back are by getting involved in trail maintenance, or by joining a hacking group to remove alien vegetation. If you notice erosion, broken signage or damage to the route while on a hike, stop for 10 minutes and do your best to repair (or at least arrest) the damage. After all, you have been using the trail and it is only fair to give something back. If there is a trail club in your area, they will be able to advise you regarding trail maintenance; if not, assemble some friends and do it yourself.

CLEANING UP A STREAM NOT ONLY IMPROVES THE ENVIRONMENT, IT IS A WAY OF GIVING SOMETHING BACK FOR THE PLEASURE YOU RECEIVE.

WHEN YOU GOTTA GO, YOU GOTTA GO — BUT EXTREME CLIMATES MAY CALL FOR EXTREME MEASURES. NO MATTER HOW DIFFICULT IT MAY BE TO ACCOMPLISH, BE SURE TO RESPECT THE ENVIRONMENT AT ALL TIMES, EVEN WHEN IT MAY NOT BE RESPECTING YOU!

What to do with waste

■ ORGANIC MATTER Fruit and vegetable leftovers are decomposable, but may attract animals which could easily become camp site pests. Bury degradable waste to a minimum depth of 15cm (6in) or pack (carry) it out. Citrus peels take years to biodegrade and will therefore be an eyesore to others, so pack these out.

■ CIGARETTE BUTTS This is littering at its worst. Culprits are guilty of polluting the fresh air, leaving behind litter that takes years to bio-degrade and create a potential fire hazard. If you simply have to smoke on a hike, keep a small container on hand and take your cigarette butts home (a film canister is ideal).

■ HUMAN WASTE Bears may do it in the woods, but this does not give you carte blanche to indiscriminately use the outdoors as your personal loo. The proper way is to take a spade and dig a trench approximately 30cm (12in) deep, do your thing, add a sprinkle of stove fuel and ignite to burn the toilet paper before covering it all up. Take great care when igniting stove fuel and ensure the fire is properly extinguished before you move away. You must be at least 100m (110yds) away from any water source, so start climbing if you are in a canyon. In extreme climates, if you can't dig through snow or ice, your only option is to pack it out, so think this through beforehand.

■ TAMPONS Take along some zip-lock bags. Seal used sanitary pads or tampons inside a double bag and pack them out.

■ PLASTIC AND TIN If you are in any doubt as to whether something will biodegrade, pack it out. Don't try to burn tin foil as you will simply end up burying it under the ashes from where it will resurface after a while as messy litter.

Current hiking philosophy embraces the principles of minimum-impact hiking, so be prepared to pack out whatever you pack in. A sad fact is that responsible hikers are often forced to remove waste left by less ethical trail users.

When buying equipment, try to select 'green' products, checking on aspects such as labour practices and the use of recycled material in both manufacture and packaging.

Use biodegradable soap or shampoo when bathing or doing the dishes, to prevent contaminating the ground, and always remember to wash at least 100m (110yds) from any water source.

When urinating, step off the trail and move well away from a water source, where you can limit any damage to terrain (and avoid cat calls from fellow hikers), enjoying the view while you go.

Being environmentally responsible, or 'green', extends to an awareness of everything you do in the outdoors, such as pulling up invasive vegetation, or not taking short cuts that could result in erosion. At all times, try to monitor your overall impact on the trail.

ALWAYS REMEMBER THE IMPORTANCE OF BEING ENVIRONMENTALLY AWARE AROUND RIVER COURSES, OR WHEN TEMPTED TO TAKE SHORT CUTS.

Gearing up

going shopping will be, in many respects, your first expedition and you need to plan as you would for a multi-day hiking trip. Identify in advance the specific gear items you will require, check which retailers carry stock of these and, most importantly, set yourself a realistic budget. Initial internet research is always helpful and, when you set off, take along a check list on which you can compare prices, payment terms, features, guarantees or warranties and after-sales service.

above FIELD GUIDES AND BINOCULARS MAY SEEM LIKE LUXURIES, BUT TO A KEEN NATURALIST, THEY MIGHT BE ESSENTIAL ITEMS.

opposite THE AMOUNT OF GEAR REQUIRED ON A HIKE CAN APPEAR EXCESSIVE, BUT BEING PROPERLY EQUIPPED AND WELL PREPARED MAKES ANY HIKING TRIP A PLEASURABLE EXPERIENCE.

Basic gear requirements

The gear you pack depends very much on where, when and what you are planning. Although the amount of kit you take on a short hike will be less than that required for a multi-day trip, the basics are essentially the same. To simplify preparations, outdoor equipment and supplies may be divided into six main categories: pack system, apparel, shelter, utensils, first aid, sleeping kit and food, all of which are described below and covered in more detail during the course of this chapter.

1. BACKPACK OR RUCKSACK This is a top priority, as it will have to carry all your provisions and kit for the duration of your hike. It therefore needs to be the right dimensions for the job, as well as for your individual body geometry and weight-carrying ability.

2. CLOTHING This includes footwear, head-gear and any special items required for extreme weather. When considering what to include, take into account factors such as prevailing weather, route distance and terrain.

3. SHELTER Your portable home must be able to shelter and protect you from the elements. The precise size, shape and specifications will depend on factors such as the weather conditions you expect to encounter and how many people it needs to accommodate.

4. UTENSILS AND FIRST AID This broad category covers everything you will require for cooking, eating, assistance with walking, safety and survival, first aid, navigation and ad hoc activities, such as bird watching or identifying plants along the route.

5. SLEEPING KIT The rating (warmth factor) of your sleeping bag and the type of mattress you choose will be determined by the minimum temperatures you expect to experience on the trail.

6. FOOD You may have the best gear money can buy, but it will mean nothing if you don't fuel your body with the right food and enough liquid on a daily basis. Skimp on something else, but never on food or water, and always ensure you have emergency supplies.

Pack systems

A wide range of pack systems is available to suit every outdoor activity, from one-day or overnight hikes to multi-day expeditions. The bottom line is that size does matter, so make this your primary consideration. Once you have determined the required volume (the actual internal size of the pack), consider stability, comfort, durability and weight. The technical fit of your pack is as important as that of your boots, so always ensure that its shape and design suits your individual anatomical proportions.

The good news is that it is a buyers' market, with many manufacturers offering competitive product ranges featuring the latest in rip-stop fabrics, air-flow backs, hydration add-ons, shock-cord carrying systems and tensioning straps. Take your chosen pack on a test run if the retailer will oblige, opting for a snug body fit and easy access without restricting your movements.

Day packs

Day tripping does not necessitate you being a beast of burden, with the average pack volume for short trips hovering somewhere between 10 and 35 litres (2 and 8 gallons). Either opt for a hip pack (a small pack with a broad hip-belt, a main compartment and two bottle holders) or a more regular shoulder pack configuration.

Versatility will go a long way towards satisfying your trail needs; a shock-cord carrying system, mesh or fabric side pockets and sufficient storage space will enable you to use the same pack for mountain biking and other activities. If you have another larger pack for longer hikes, then a compatible hydration system is an advantage. On packs that are not waterproof, a handy feature to look for is an elasticized, built-in splash cover to protect your gear during heavy rain; it can also come in handy when floating your pack across a lake or stream.

Keep your body cool by going for a back system incorporating mesh or tunnelling, thus allowing airflow between the pack and your back. Construction should be durable and light, utilizing high performance and hard-wearing fabrics, with well-padded shoulder straps allowing all-day comfort. Colour is a personal choice. Bright yellows and reds allow high visibility during emergency situations, but the general trend is towards earthy hues that blend in with nature.

DAY PACKS ARE OFTEN MULTI-FUNCTIONAL, SO MAKE SURE THAT YOURS MEETS A RANGE OF NEEDS.

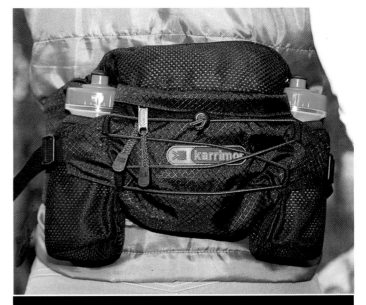

A HIP PACK WILL BE SUFFICIENT FOR SHORT HIKES, PARTICULARLY IN THOSE EARLY DAYS WHEN YOU ARE TRYING TO GET YOUR LEGS ACCUSTOMED TO WALKING.

THE LONGER THE TRAIL, THE BIGGER THE PACK, BUT NEVER SET OFF WITH MORE THAN YOU CAN COMFORTABLY CARRY, AS THE PACK WILL SOON WEIGH DOWN BOTH YOUR BODY AND SPIRIT.

A PACK COVER IS USEFUL WHEN IT RAINS. IT CAN ALSO PROTECT YOUR BACKPACK FROM DEW AT NIGHT IF THERE IS NO ROOM FOR IT IN THE TENT.

Expedition backpacks

The longer the trail, the bigger the pack. Although this generalization makes some sense, there are obvious limits to what the human body can comfortably carry. Many factors, including all-round fitness, endurance, altitude, trail distance and your own body size will determine your personal load limitation.

As a rule of thumb, start with 20 per cent of your body weight, gradually working up to 30 per cent or whatever you feel comfortable with. The heavier your pack, the more important its fit and balance will be. Begin by selecting the right frame. Although some external frames distribute weight more efficiently, an internal frame is more suitable for a variety of trail environments, as it has a lower centre of gravity and is better for carrying heavy loads.

Once you have decided on a suitable volume and frame, make sure that the pack offers easy access on the trail. Your best option is a pack with two main compartments, a selection of expanding side pockets and mesh compartments, and a high spindrift collar.

Other handy features include a zip-off hip pack which converts into a separate day pack, an internal zip converting the two main compartments into one, pole sheaths and compression straps.

The carry system is just as important, so look for a well-padded, broad hip belt, a shaped and padded shoulder harness and a well-ventilated back with a solid lumbar pad. A clip-lock chest strap (to keep the carry harness from pulling your shoulders back), expandable gussets and a user-friendly hydration system add further value.

A double layer of water-resistant material at the base of the pack helps prevent moisture seeping in when the pack is placed on the ground and adds to its overall durability. If the pack does not come fitted with a splash cover, purchase an additional, elasticized rain cover as insurance against getting your gear wet.

Make sure you can make adjustments to the pack as you walk, thus avoiding time-wasting stop-starts. Finally, there's the nitty-gritty of fabric, colour, durability, after-sales service and, of course, price.

Front view

A - SIDE POCKETS Size may be adjusted with compression straps.

B - EQUIPMENT STRAPS For attaching ice axes, shovels or other tools for convenient access. (Also called daisy chain loops.)

C - SPINDRIFT COLLAR (COWL) Protects contents against rain or snow. Extends above the main compartment and is closed with a drawstring (see illustration).

D - COMPRESSION STRAPS These run vertically and horizontally and are used to compress the volume of the pack to suit your load (see illustration).

E - BOTTOM (LOWER) COMPARTMENT A front zipper makes it easier to access items. A double-layered base keeps the pack dry when on the ground.

F - OUTSIDE POCKETS Expandable storage pockets for wet, messy or constant-use items. May be made of mesh.

G - BELT POCKET Perfect for storing keys, money and small items you may need to keep safe and be able to access easily.

Back view

A - SHOULDER HARNESS
Wide, padded shoulder straps offer maximum comfort.

B - BACK SYSTEM Provides a ventilation tunnel with breathable mesh material to allow air to circulate.

C - LUMBAR PAD Protects the base of the spine.

D - HIP BELT Thick padding protects your hips when carrying a heavy load.

E - VERTICAL ADJUSTMENT STRAP Used to lower or raise the vertical position of the pack in relation to the harness.

F - LOAD-LIFTER TABS Also called stabilizer straps. Can be adjusted to lift or lower the pack's centre of gravity on your back.

G - WAIST STRAP Links the hip pads across the waist for added stability and load distribution.

H - GRAB HANDLE Convenient handhold for lifting or carrying the backpack (see illustration).

I - INTERNAL FRAME (not shown). Usually made from lightweight aluminium (in some packs the frame can be custom-bent to fit body contours).

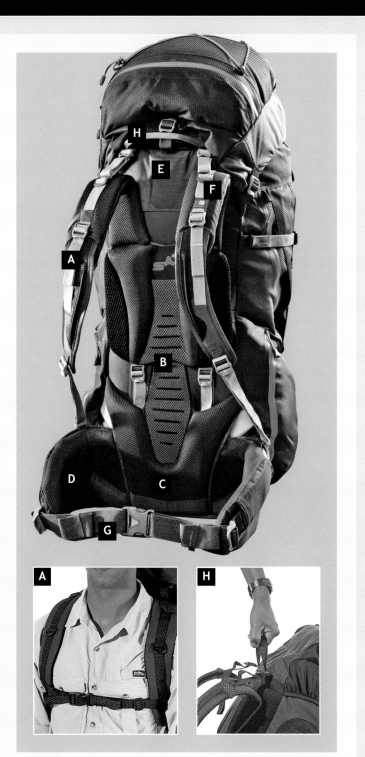

Dressing for the great outdoors

Clothing

Dress sense on a hiking trip has more to do with practicalities than with making a fashion statement. Increased specialization in outdoor garments has resulted in an abundance of high-performance fabrics, such as Gore-Tex, Pertex, Tactel, Polartec and Entropy. These technical micro-fibres ensure multi-functional adventure wear that is able to cope with a variety of extreme outdoor conditions without compromising on weight, breathability, insulation or durability.

Layering is the new cold weather doctrine, and this cannot be stressed enough when protecting yourself against the elements. A close-fitting base layer acts as a conduit to wick (channel) moisture away from the skin, thus allowing sweat to evaporate without cooling the body. The middle layer is thermodynamically constructed to allow maximum comfort, heat retention and stretch without adding too much bulk or weight, thus controlling body temperature. Finally, there is a durable and windproof outer layer, sometimes called a shell, to protect you against the wind (this garment is usually waterproof or water-resistant as well).

Body extremities (your feet, hands and head) are vulnerable to cold, so thermal socks, gloves, scarves and beanies should be an integral part of your armour.

Extreme heat can be as harmful as cold, and high temperatures necessitate quick-drying breathable fabrics that help to regulate your core temperature. In regions where the sun is strong, cover as much of your body as possible, and wear a wide-brimmed hat and sunglasses to protect your face and eyes. Some leading manufacturers of outdoor clothing now incorporate a built-in ultraviolet (UV) shield in their fabrics.

Footwear

Obviously terrain, climate and distance will influence what you wear on your feet, but basically it comes down to personal choice. You can choose between approach shoes, all-terrain trail runners, hiking sandals and a huge variety of boots. Style does count, but is always secondary to weight and a good fit. Where possible, try on footwear before you buy it.

With boots, ample padding on the tongue and in the foot-bed will add to a comfortable fit, while flexible uppers and a sturdy heel grip will improve general foot support. A protective rand (strip), rubberized toe box

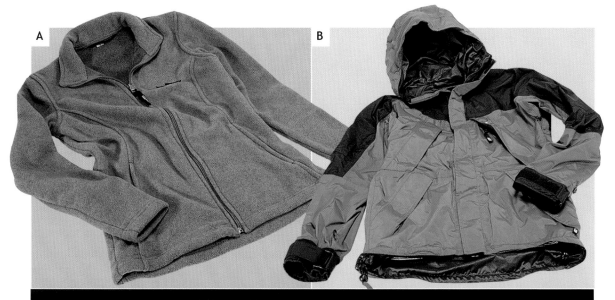

THIS MID-LAYER FLEECE (A) AND WINDPROOF SHELL JACKET (B) ARE EXAMPLES OF NEW GENERATION HIKING GEAR. MODERN TECHNOLOGY HAS PRODUCED A WIDE RANGE OF FABRICS AND MATERIALS THAT ARE WARMER AND LIGHTER, DRY FASTER AND LOOK BETTER THAN EVER BEFORE.

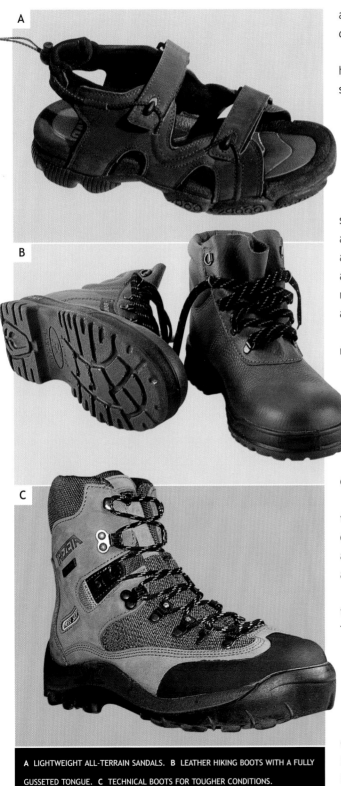

A LIGHTWEIGHT ALL-TERRAIN SANDALS. B LEATHER HIKING BOOTS WITH A FULLY GUSSETED TONGUE. C TECHNICAL BOOTS FOR TOUGHER CONDITIONS.

and hard-wearing outer-sole will make the shoe durable enough to cope with harsh terrain.

Light trail use (think easy day or overnight hikes) allows for experimentation with approach shoes and hybrid trainers. These offer minimum support, but break in easily, dry quickly and are very affordable.

On longer, but less-demanding trails, you may opt for a light boot, possibly combining leather with breathable modern synthetic materials in the uppers, but offering less support and durability. Even though these boots are not all that waterproof, they dry quickly and are not too expensive. Look for features such as a fully gusseted tongue, which makes the boot more water-resistant and prevents the irritating accumulation of trail debris inside your boot.

Long distance hikes involving rough or jagged rocks, thick snow or hard ice require heavy-duty, technical boots with high-quality leather uppers, a non-slip, reinforced sole and good ankle and bridge support. If you are hiking in extremely cold conditions, choose boots with as few seams as possible (to make them virtually watertight), compatibility with crampons and additional insulation.

If you can, carry two sets of complimentary footwear, swopping boots for all-terrain sandals or trainers for specific sections or around camp, as this will not only preserve your boots but will also give your feet a well-deserved break.

Wearing good socks is as important as having the right shoes, so test them before long hikes. Thick socks may cause blisters through bunching and moisture retention, but they work well for some walkers. Dual-layered socks offer a durable, woven outer layer and a breathable inner layer which assists in moisture control while minimizing friction, thereby reducing chafing and blisters. When wearing sandals in hot conditions, it is possible to go without socks, but beware of thorns and sharp stones, and use sun block on the tops of your feet.

Extreme heat

Headgear
Broad-brimmed, ventilated hat to assist in temperature control. A chin strap or cord that is used to secure it to clothing is a handy feature in windy areas.

Glasses
Polarizing lenses with wrap-around frames protect eyes from grit and sun damage (UV rays) and prevent them from drying out in warm, windy conditions.

Shirt or top
Loose fitting and light-coloured to reflect heat, in lightweight, breathable and quick-drying material. Built-in ultraviolet (UV) protection is an added benefit.

Pants
Active zip-off longs (easily convertible to shorts) in a lightweight, breathable and quick-drying material, preferably with deep pockets — style is a personal choice.

Footwear
Lightweight boots, ventilated river or all-terrain sandals, or trainers and lightweight quick-drying socks (if preferred).

BUILT-IN ZIPS CLEVERLY TURN LONG TROUSERS INTO SHORTS.

Extreme cold

Headgear
A jacket hood keeps you dry, while a long-necked balaclava worn underneath helps to improve heat retention and protects against the wind (not shown).

Glasses
Wrap-around frame with lenses that offer total protection from snow glare and reflection as well as UV rays.

Shirt or top
Layered approach with long-sleeved base layer to wick moisture, mid-layer fleece for insulation and a rain- and windproof outer shell. A close-fitting adjustable hood stops wind or water penetrating the outer layer. A poncho is a good alternative to a raincoat, but can become unwieldy in very windy weather.

Pants
Alpine salopets or Pathfinder-style over-trousers in Microtex/Polar-guard combination. Pants must be water-resistant and insulated, with scuff patches and articulated knees to allow ease of movement.

Footwear
Technical boots with high, insulated uppers and Gore-Tex socks, plus gaiters to keep out snow and moisture.

USE A PONCHO TO COVER YOU AND YOUR PACK WHEN IT RAINS.

ALPINE-STYLE SALOPETS ARE IDEAL IN SNOW.

Choosing a shelter

Next to your backpack and sleeping bag, your tent will be one of the most expensive items on your outdoor shopping list. Deciding factors will be cost (relative to your budget), weight (always a trade-off against price), size (how many people it must accommodate), and likely weather conditions.

You will best know your own budget and, to a large extent, the carry weight of your tent will vary inversely with what you are prepared to pay. Size therefore becomes the primary issue, with expected weather conditions playing an extremely important role when it comes to deciding on the technical specifications.

Tents

Step into any outdoor retail store and you will be confronted by an array of tent shapes, styles, colours and fabrics. A useful feature to consider is ease of erection. Will you be able to pitch the tent when it is blowing a gale? Other considerations are whether it offers enough storage space for your packs; whether you can sit up comfortably, or stretch out without getting your nose wedged in a zip; and whether poles and pegs are lightweight.

The more breathable the tent material is, the less condensation you will have to cope with when it is zipped up to keep the cold out. Finally, make sure that the screen netting covering the openings is fine enough to keep out mosquitos, midges and other insects. Take your time; insist on seeing the tent pitched, crawl inside and check it out. Remember, when you are out in the wilderness, this will be your home.

MODERN TENTS ARE EASY TO PUT UP, BREATHABLE AND LIGHTWEIGHT, AS WELL AS OFFERING GOOD STABILITY IN ADVERSE WEATHER CONDITIONS.

Size and shape

Do you need a one-man tent or will there be more of you huddling together? If you're going solo, opt for a bivy shelter or lightweight tent, both of which offer a reasonable combination of space and rigidity.

The outdated A-frame design (also known as a ridge or pup tent) requires anchor lines to be properly pitched and has little to offer except affordability.

The dome-shaped, or geodesic tent, arguably the most popular option, is a freestanding tent with ample space and

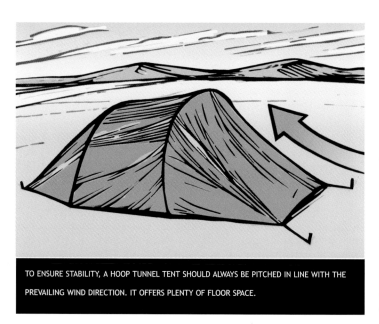

TO ENSURE STABILITY, A HOOP TUNNEL TENT SHOULD ALWAYS BE PITCHED IN LINE WITH THE PREVAILING WIND DIRECTION. IT OFFERS PLENTY OF FLOOR SPACE.

A GEODESIC TENT OFFERS GOOD SLEEPING AND STORAGE SPACE. THE FRONT PORTAL CAN BE USED TO STOW YOUR BACKPACK AND ALSO PROVIDES SHELTER FOR A COOKING STOVE DURING INCLEMENT WEATHER. GUY ROPES (A) AID STABILITY; WHILE INTERNAL INSULATION (B) IS A MUST IN COLD WEATHER.

good stability in the wind. Erection is based on a multi-pole system and the tent's weight to space ratio is good, although ventilation and sloping walls (in some designs) can be a problem. A variety of geodesic configurations is available from a range of reputable international manufacturers.

The hoop, or tunnel tent has the advantage of rectangular floor space, nearly vertical side walls, optimum stability when pitched in line with the prevailing wind direction and an excellent weight to internal-size ratio.

Grading tents by usage

Terminology regarding tents can be quite confusing, so here is a quick list of terms for your reference. Single-wall construction refers to the lack of a fly sheet (an additional covering stretched over the tent to form an outer roof); expect to do battle with both heat and cold due to the lack of proper insulation.

A summer tent is a lightweight shelter meant for mild weather and offers protection against little more than the insects buzzing about on a temperate night.

A three-season tent incorporates screened canopies, fly-sheets and a ventilation system able to handle most conditions short of heavy northern hemisphere winters.

What sets the four-season tent apart is its ability to shed snow and to handle higher wind speeds. Loosely grouped together under the term technical tents, four-season tents are preferred by mountaineering or climbing parties heading into extreme conditions. These tents may feature Gore-Tex or similar fabrics instead of nylon, plus heavy-duty industrial stitching, a coated base, lap-felled (taped) seams, carbon-fibre poles and superior workmanship.

Sleeping bags

One tip before you snuggle into the down-filled territory of sleeping bags; remember that at night, most of the chill sneaks up through the ground, so get some insulation between you and mother earth. Choose either a closed-cell (compressed) foam pad or a self-inflating air mattress. Closed-cell foam pads are cheaper and come in a range of densities and thicknesses, offering varying levels of comfort and insulation. Self-inflating air mattresses (air beds) are prone to the occasional puncture, with obvious consequences. Cheaper versions tend to be quite bulky, but they do promise a comfortable night.

Your sleeping bag is another high-cost item on your shopping list, but keep in mind that you will be spending as much (if not more) time in the bag than you will on your feet! Without a comfortable night's sleep, a hiking trip can turn out to be sheer torture, so buy the best you can afford. Cost is only one of many considerations though; temperature rating, pack-down size, weight and usage life being other factors.

Many of these factors are dependent on the type of bag filling, with the market basically divided between natural down (feathers) and synthetic fibres. Although down offers excellent warmth to weight ratio and superior breathability, the new generation of synthetic fibres is hard to beat and will out-perform down when wet, while also drying much faster. Hollow fibre and continuous fibre (which does not break apart during washing or use) enable some manufacturers' fillings to trap more air, making for warmer bags without compromising on weight and size.

Temperature ratings identify the range within which the manufacturer claims the sleeping bag will operate at optimum performance. A bag rated -12°–5°C (10°– 40°F), for example, should handle temperatures (measured in windless conditions) in that range, but if you feel the cold easily, err on the side of caution. Sleeping in woollen hats, thermal underwear and socks or using a thermal sleeping bag-liner all contribute to increasing your bag's rating if an unexpected cold snap sets in. An internal liner offers the added advantage of keeping your bag clean, which means fewer trips to the laundry and a significant increase in its usage life.

Features to consider before buying a sleeping bag (other than the stuffing), are a fitted, drawstring hood, which helps stop heat loss through your head, anti-snag zips with a lifelong guarantee, a full baffle to enhance insulation, and a shoulder collar to trap warm air inside. A zipped bottom vent allows air flow on those warmer nights, while a double-layered foot-bed will also contribute to the bag's versatility and durability.

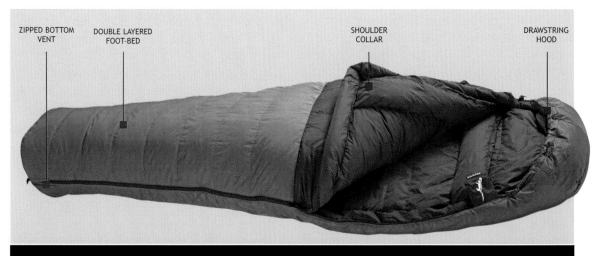

ZIPPED BOTTOM VENT   DOUBLE LAYERED FOOT-BED   SHOULDER COLLAR   DRAWSTRING HOOD

A GOOD SLEEPING BAG IS A LONG-TERM INVESTMENT, SO BUY THE BEST YOU CAN AFFORD, OPTING FOR ONE THAT SUITS YOUR HEIGHT AND BUILD, AS WELL AS HAVING FEATURES SUITABLE FOR THE TYPE OF CONDITIONS IN WHICH YOU ARE LIKELY TO HIKE.

Camping without a tent

above A GROUNDSHEET IS BETTER THAN NOTHING IF YOU GET CAUGHT IN THE RAIN.

right A BIVY BAG IS AN OPTION FOR A SHORT HIKE IN MILD WEATHER.

off as little more than a large plastic bag. As the price increases you get the added benefit of breathable nylon fabric (such as Gore-Tex), anchored foot and head domes, a laminated floor and mesh netting to keep insects out. The bivy bag's greatest advantage is its weight (often weighing in at less than 1kg (2 lb), but it does not leave you with any space to store your kit. Because of its size, it may generate excessive internal condensation. On the whole, a bivy will serve as an adequate shelter for spartan hikers, but only in summer or in the most temperate conditions.

If you are weight and space conscious and are prepared to get really close to nature, a bivy (bivouac) bag might do the trick. These are lightweight, waterproof and compact, but fail to score many points in the comfort stakes.

A bivy basically acts as an outside shell to your sleeping bag, with the most basic models starting

Make sure you fit the bag comfortably (ignoring any comments from other shoppers as you test-drive it on the shop floor!). Tall people need to make sure their shoulders will be adequately covered, so testing the bag is worth a few smiles from other customers. A small inner pocket (for keeping keys, money or glasses secure) is a handy addition, as is the option of zipping ('mating') your bag to another.

Between hikes, never store your sleeping bag compressed inside its stuff bag; rather allow the micro-fibre stuffing to expand, thus maintaining its natural fluff and ability to trap air. When washing or cleaning your sleeping bag, follow the manufacturer's instructions to the letter.

A SELF-INFLATING MATTRESS WILL INSULATE YOU FROM COLD SEEPING UP FROM THE GROUND AND ADD A MODICUM OF COMFORT TO YOUR NIGHTS.

Equipment and accessories

You will find many tools of the trail useful in helping you cope with outdoor life. Space is the final arbiter, but always pack the core kit items featured below, dividing them between the group where possible.

HEAD TORCH Lights up your life when it gets dark, leaving your hands free for more important things. A long burn time, comfortable head strap and powerful beam are the most important criteria. Some models are waterproof, and most feature either tungsten or energy efficient light emitting diodes (LEDs), with the latter lasting for weeks. (A tiny solar panel and rechargeable batteries are great for long hikes).

WHISTLE If you get lost, a whistle is more effective than shouting when trying to guide in a search party. Buy a good quality whistle of the type used in sports, rather than relying on a child's toy or a relic from a festive season cracker.

FOLDING SPADE It needs to be light, sturdy and functional enough to do the job when you want to do yours. It is a good idea to store it in a plastic bag or bin liner, to avoid transferring dirt to other items in your backpack.

LANTERN Handy when you want soft diffused light inside the tent or while cooking outside. Butane gas lanterns work well, but may not be allowed on some aircraft due to safety concerns. Long-burn battery candles with diffusing attachments, candle lanterns and light sticks are other options.

LIGHTER One of the easiest items to forget if you're a non-smoker. Waterproof matches are another option, but always make sure at least two people have the means to start a fire.

MESS KIT Choose stainless steel or lightweight aluminium comprising two pans (with stable, fold-out handles), plates and cutlery all contained in a stuff bag. Coffee and tea are well-deserved luxuries on the trail, so include an unbreakable mug. Don't forget washing-up liquid and pot scourers.

MULTI-TOOL OR POCKET KNIFE Why take a knife when you can take a pocket toolkit? There are many options available, with a wide range of functions, but if weight is a factor, restrict yourself to tools that are really necessary, such as a can opener, a sharp blade, scissors and a small screwdriver.

PERSONAL TOILETRIES AND FIRST-AID KIT Fill small, zipped bags with whatever you think you can't live without (toilet paper is good; remove the inner cardboard cylinder and flatten it to take up less space). Pack insect repellent as part of your stash. A basic personal first-aid kit is essential for treating minor problems. Include prescription medication and whatever else you require to treat pre-existing conditions. At least one member of the group should carry a properly equipped medical kit to deal with more serious emergencies. (See also pp78–81.)

STOVES There are many options, so first decide on the type of fuel. Methylated spirit (denatured alcohol) burners are solid, safe and reliable, but quite big. Disposable butane canister models (as shown) are affordable and small, but you're stuck if you run out of gas on the trail (and you have to carry all those empty canisters home). Multi-fuel stoves burn on just about any fuel, but need cleaning, pack a hefty price and require you to carry a fuel bottle. Consider the duration and nature of your hike before you choose.

WATER PURIFIER It's what's inside that counts. The filter elements are usually made of carbon, ceramic, fibreglass or a combination of these (absolute pore size indicates which micro-organisms won't get through the filter). Purifiers use gravity feed, a squeeze bottle, or a pump mechanism during operation and are best used in conjunction with purifying tablets. It is worth researching a range of models before making your purchase.

HIKING POLES These have become an indispensable accessory for most serious hikers, allowing the arms and shoulders to bear a proportionate amount of upper body weight while simultaneously stabilizing you when moving across treacherous terrain. Advanced pole designs incorporate a built-in, spring-loaded shock absorber to minimize jarring and wrist stress. Use singly or in pairs.

COMPASS OR GPS Pack at least one compass (left) or GPS (below left) per group when venturing into the unknown. You may lose your printed trail guide or stray from the group, or the only person who knows the route may be injured, leaving you to lead the group to safety. Make sure you know how they work and have spare batteries. An accurate map of the area and a pencil are essential for plotting your course. (See also pp76–77.)

CAMERA What's the use of trekking to the peaks of Nepal if you don't have the photographs to prove you were there? Amateur photographers need nothing more than a digital zoom compact, but should also pack ample batteries and enough memory cards.

LENGTH OF ROPE This has unlimited uses, from crossing ravines to splinting a broken leg. Carry 10m (30ft) of quality climbing rope with a minimum 5mm (1/4in) diameter.

BINOCULARS These are a necessity if you're a keen birder or game viewer, but are also useful for assessing terrain in remote or unfamiliar areas. Choose from the many compact yet powerful models available.

FIELD GUIDES Enjoy nature more by recognizing and identifying some of the plants and creatures you are sharing it with. Weight and space are always an issue, so try to find paperback or abridged versions.

Food

When planning menus, weight, bulk, nutritional value and personal preference are the obvious criteria to consider and it is here that dried, freeze-dried or dehydrated foods score high marks. Pack ample natural foods, like raisins, nuts and dried fruit, as well as energy bars, soups, isotonic drink mixes, powdered milk, instant mashed potato and dehydrated soya mince. These foods all have high nutritional values and are reasonably easy to prepare, although dehydrated powders require sufficient water.

Although dehydrated and freeze-dried meals are handy, they can be quite expensive. Tinned (canned) foods are easy to prepare, but add weight and bulk, so restrict them to one or two luxury items.

Preplan your meals on a day-to-day basis, packing food for each day separately in order to avoid over-indulging during the first few days, only to be left with black tea and dry biscuits to sustain you during the remainder of the hike.

Varying your food is important, as this helps to provide all the nutrients you need to sustain you, particularly on a multi-day hike.

Always pack enough provisions to last beyond your expected resupply points. On even the most rugged trails, chances are that there will be a food source within shouting distance at any time. It might not be a supermarket with wide aisles and stocked fridges, but staples like bread, rice or beans, as well as fruit and vegetables, fish or meat are usually available from village stores or directly from the local people. However, unless you know an area well, it is best not to depend on obtaining fresh provisions. Rather, use them to supplement your rations and boost your spirits.

Chapter 4 has more information on menu-planning and meeting your body's energy needs.

RE-SUPPLYING WITH FRESH PRODUCE ON THE GROUND IS ALWAYS AN OPTION, BUT UNLESS YOU KNOW AN AREA WELL DO NOT DEPEND ON IT. ALWAYS CARRY ENOUGH FOOD TO SEE YOU THROUGH.

Doing your first hike

It might have taken a few weeks of dedicated retail therapy, but you are now all geared up to go walkabout. If you're planning a group outing, arrange an informal gathering of all participants and identify a day or overnight hike in the immediate area that is agreeable to everyone. Utilize the get-together to discuss group responsibilities, assigning specific tasks to various members. Exchange phone numbers and decide on an easily identifiable meeting place.

A check list is the easiest way to make sure that group members are clear on their duties, permitting you to tick off specific tasks upon completion. If you plan to hike solo or with just one companion, all these tasks will be your responsibility and you need to be extra careful, as you will have no backup on the trail.

Short hike check list

Entry fees and permits: Is an entry fee required and are you able to pay at the start of the trail? Some hiking permits need to be procured from the offices of relevant authorities situated in another town or city.

Food: Take enough food for your planned meals, as well as sufficient emergency rations to last you through the night if you should get lost.

Water: Take a minimum of 2 litres (4pt) of water per person per day, even if there are water points on the trail. The body's water requirements vary, depending on the temperature and the level of exercise, but expect to drink about 1 litre (2pt) for every two hours spent along the route.

Weather forecast: Get a weather forecast covering the duration of your hike and, if possible, find out what the weather was like during the week preceding your visit. This will help you contend with unexpected conditions when you arrive at your destination.

Clothing: Never trust the weather report completely and always take along a compact raincoat, cap or hat, thermal top and a space (emergency) blanket just in case. If you expect your shoes to get wet, it is a good idea to carry an extra pair.

Shelter: Trails with a single overnight stop normally have permanent, well-maintained huts or chalets, usually with ablution and cooking facilities, but you will need a sleeping bag. Determine beforehand what is provided so that you don't carry more than is necessary or leave something essential behind.

Responsibility areas

- NAVIGATION Sourcing of maps, compass, GPS and navigational aids; pre-plotting of coordinates.
- RATIONS Menu planning, purchase, packing and distribution of food and emergency rations.
- ADMINISTRATION Access permission, permits, passports, paperwork, travel arrangements.
- COMMUNICATION/INFORMATION Contact numbers, emergency procedures, trail research, guidebooks or field guides.
- PROVISIONS Specialist gear required, shared gear, final check lists, garbage control.
- EMERGENCIES Flares, radio, mirror, long-term weather forecast, security, emergency numbers.
- MEDICAL Relevant first aid qualification, first aid kit, vaccination info, specific health risks.
- PATHFINDING Lead walker, good directional, hiking and natural skills; could be group leader.
- EXPERTS Geology, fauna and flora, astronomy, field identification manuals, binoculars.
- CARRIERS Strong physique, good endurance, pack to body-weight ratio, sense of humour.

HILLS, VALLEYS AND AREAS OF NATURAL BEAUTY CLOSE TO TOWNS OR URBAN CENTRES MAKE IDEAL VENUES FOR DAY HIKES.

WHEN YOU ARRIVE AT THE STARTING POINT, DOUBLE-CHECK YOUR PACKS AND GEAR BEFORE SETTING OUT.

First aid: Pack an approved first aid kit covering all eventualities you may encounter along your route. Contents should be checked to make sure that no medical products are out of date.

Telephone: Take a mobile phone if you know you will be within signal range — chances are it could save your life in an emergency situation, but don't spoil the serenity of nature for others by chatting constantly.

Sun protection: Shielding yourself against the sun's ultraviolet (UV) rays is imperative, so pack sun block, lip salve and protective clothing.

Emergency procedures: Plan beforehand what you will do in case of an emergency and ensure you have the necessary contact numbers on hand. Notify someone trustworthy of your estimated return time so they can contact the authorities if something goes wrong. Pack a lighter or waterproof matches.

Maps and guides: If the route is not well marked, you might require a map or the services of a guide or an experienced hiker who knows the trail well. Most short hikes do not require additional navigation aids.

Land access: Unless hiking on a designated trail, never assume you have access to a specific section of land. Contact the relevant local authority, land owner or regulatory body to find out about access requirements.

Extras: Items that can make a hike more memorable include cameras, binoculars and field guides, so take them at your own discretion. Don't forget sunglasses, toilet paper and a spade or trowel!

Choosing your route

For the moment, you will be planning a day or overnight hike on a well-signposted route. This does not mean that you should not plan, as things can go wrong, even on a controlled trail. Choose your destination with your party's weakest walker in mind, ascertaining that they are able to cope with the terrain, temperature and altitude expected along the way.

The preferred rucksack volume used on most day hikes varies between 15 and 30 litres (3 and 6 gallons), giving you ample packing space. There are only two basic packing rules: pack heavier items at the bottom of your pack, and pack items you'll need during the hike in an easily accessible place. Avoid placing objects with hard edges or points where they will dig into your back and cause discomfort or bruising. Knives, scissors or any sharp objects should be securely packed to ensure your safety during a fall or bump. Place keys and other jangly items between clothing to avoid constant noise irritation.

If you are venturing out in wet weather, you need to keep the contents of your day pack dry. Forget about packs being waterproof; with all the zips and stitching, most manufacturers will promise water-resistance at best. Some packs do however come with a nifty little attachment called a splash cover. This waterproof sheet with elasticized edges can be used to rain-proof your pack when the heavens open up so that the contents stay dry. If you want to make doubly sure, line the inside of your bag with a pack liner or a plastic garbage bag to enhance waterproofing.

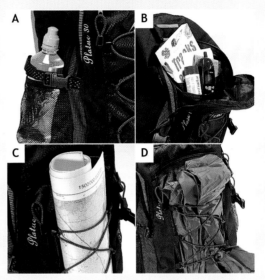

■ HYDRATION SYSTEM Most day-packs come with an insulated bladder sleeve, thus keeping your water cool and enabling on-the-move drinking. Choose a well-made bladder and locking bite valve to avoid leaks. Squeeze bottles also work well and may be kept in the pack's side pockets for easy access. **(A)**

■ MAIN COMPARTMENT Heavy items that won't be continually required can go at the bottom of the pack (extra water, food, safety equipment, first aid kit and a second pair of shoes). Add a small stove if you plan to have tea, coffee or cooked food along the way.

■ SIDE POCKETS These are easily reached without taking the pack off your back. These mesh or fabric pockets with elasticized rim bands are perfect for stashing squeeze water bottles, but they also provide handy storage space for snacks or a compact camera.

■ TOP POCKET Use this to stow items that will be used regularly as you progress along the hike, but which also need to stay dry.

Maps, hiking permits, mobile phone (switched off), binoculars, field guides and insect repellent all qualify. **(B)**

■ SHOCK-CORD CARRYING SYSTEM Often used to secure a cycle helmet, but it also works for a wet raincoat, rolled up laminated maps or similar items that do not quite fit in your pack. Items are easily lost when carried like this, so make sure they are well-secured. **(C & D)**

■ POLE POCKETS Slip hiking poles or a camera mono-pod into these for easy accessibility when you need them.

■ SPLASH COVER A stowable splash cover is usually situated in a zipped pocket near the base. Use it to cover your pack when it rains, thus keeping the contents dry. A heavy-duty garbage bag is a good stand-by.

Assist those in the group who may be struggling to keep up by carrying their packs or distributing some of their load amongst the rest of the hiking party. Never be too proud to turn back if you feel you are personally not coping; continuing might endanger your life as well as the lives of others. In order to determine the difficulty grading of a trail, you must consider factors such as the length of the trail, its environmental character and your pack weight.

Trail environments

Touch down in different parts of the world and you will find a whole host of environments varying according to the geography and climate of the region. Vegetation is determined by altitude and rainfall, while the density of foliage along sections of your route may affect your speed of advance and ability to navigate. A short hike

MOVING THROUGH DENSE VEGETATION CAN SLOW YOUR PROGRESS DRAMATICALLY AND MAY ALSO CAUSE YOU TO LOSE YOUR WAY, SO TAKE EXTRA CARE TO STICK TO THE TRAIL.

in an arid, flat environment will therefore be easier than a route through dense vegetation or one where you have to negotiate wetland marshes.

Remember that a change in weather conditions may completely alter an undemanding route in minutes: a downpour can send a raging flash-flood down a dry river bed; lightning from a thunderstorm makes rocky outcrops and ridges extremely unsafe; gale force winds make high traverses dangerous. River crossings can become hazardous if the water level is too high; if possible, wait for the water to subside to a safer level. If you absolutely have to cross, use your hiking poles or a stick to probe under the surface and to help stabilize yourself against the current. Always release your backpack's hip-belt and chest strap, so that you can shrug off the pack if you should slip and fall.

Never attempt any obstacles if you are not entirely confident that you can cope with the consequences.

Altitude

Another factor influencing route difficulty is altitude above sea level. The further you ascend, the colder it gets, with temperatures falling an average of 0.6°C (1.1°F) for every 100m (330ft) of altitude.

At higher altitudes, it becomes harder to breathe in an increasingly oxygen-starved atmosphere and you therefore need to be fitter and have higher levels of endurance to perform tasks that would be easy at a lower elevation.

You may not think you have gained much in altitude on your hike, but if you are walking on a mountain or in high country, the journey to your destination may have taken you higher than you realize. We tend to not be as aware of altitude gains when we are travelling by car, bus, train or aeroplane.

If you have a cold or chest congestion, the effects of altitude are magnified, so take extra care.

Terrain

Will you be moving along a well laid-out trail at all times or will there be some trail-blazing involved? Walking speed varies from person to person, but a reasonably fit walker can expect to cover anything

FIXED ROPES, CHAINS OR LADDERS ARE OFTEN INSTALLED TO ASSIST HIKERS WITH TOUGH SECTIONS OF THE ROUTE.

from 4–7km (3–4 miles) per hour when traversing good ground. There is no set speed though and you should always walk at a pace with which the group as a whole is comfortable. When the terrain deteriorates, distances covered will be affected. Soft sand saps your energy, rocks and stones are difficult to negotiate, snow conceals many dangers, and marshes or swamps may have to be bypassed. Sometimes handrails, chain ladders or steps may have been installed at difficult points but, on the whole, any unstable or treacherous terrain is bound to slow you down and you need to take this into account when estimating time on the trail.

Topographic height differences (or altitude gain)

If your hike includes a lot of climbs and downhills, this will further slow your walking speed. An aspect and altitude ratio diagram, or contour profile, of the route (see p16), shows a two-dimensional rendition of ascents and descents relative to distance walked and serves as a handy tool when planning your hike. Topographical maps incorporate a great deal of information, and studying the contour lines and map symbols will assist you during the planning process.

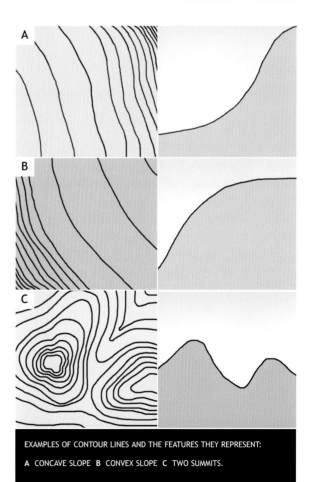

EXAMPLES OF CONTOUR LINES AND THE FEATURES THEY REPRESENT:

A CONCAVE SLOPE **B** CONVEX SLOPE **C** TWO SUMMITS.

Water

Some routes offer water replenishment points along the way, eliminating the need to carry anything but an emergency supply of at least 2 litres (4pt) per person. Ensure that water points are dependable and that the water itself is potable. Water purification tablets (these should be part of your medical kit) and a filter pump will help if water sources along the way are of a dubious standard.

Shelter and facilities

If hiking in inclement weather, determine in advance whether there are huts or other forms of shelter on the trail to shield you from rain, electric storms or strong winds. Other facilities, such as first aid stations, garbage disposal sites, refreshment stops and information kiosks at the start or at the overnight halt, or along the way, will also help to make your outing less demanding.

Along the way
Setting off

If any member of the group knows the route or area well, they should lead the way; otherwise the person with the most hiking experience should do so. Keep up a steady, yet comfortable pace, allowing sufficient time to cope with ascents along the way, and always ensure that slower walkers are able to keep up. For safety reasons, keep the hiking party together at all times; people should always be within hearing and sight distance of each other. This is especially important in misty conditions or when visibility is poor for any other reason.

Rest stops

Planning stops along your route depends on a variety of factors, including distance, walking speed, individual levels of fitness and the trail environment. Try to break the route up into manageable chunks, with regular stops at least every two hours. If you study a route

map, you might be able to identify areas of natural beauty along the way warranting these breaks.

A rock pool, waterfall, forest clearing or scenic view point will allow you to admire the scenery while getting your breath back; after all, hiking is about appreciating the splendour of wide open spaces, not about speeding through them.

Fluid intake

You have to drink while hiking, even if you don't feel thirsty. Dehydration takes place even in cool weather and it is necessary to replace the fluid your body loses naturally through breathing, perspiration and urination. Under normal hiking conditions, 3—4 litres (6—8pt) of

A RIVER OR STREAM IS A NATURAL PLACE TO STOP FOR A DRINK OR SNACK. WATER IS AVAILABLE FOR MAKING TEA, AND TIRED FEET WILL ENJOY A SOOTHING DIP.

Suggested day hike menu

On a day or an overnight hike, you have the advantage of being able to take perishable items. Have a good breakfast before setting out, as this will stand you in good stead for the first part of the day. For an overnight hike, take high-energy cereal, muesli or instant oats, and powdered or long-life milk for breakfast on the second day.

■ MORNING BREAK If you packed any fresh fruit or food items which might bruise or spoil easily, now is a good time to eat these. A muesli or granola bar and some dried fruit will also go down well. Brew a pot of tea if you have the time, or enjoy a cold drink or fruit juice if the weather is hot.

■ LUNCH Sandwiches or rolls are convenient day hike fare, so pack your own before you leave. Include instant soup or noodles for a warm pick-me-up in cold weather. An easy, although expensive option is the freeze-dried route. These complete meals are tasty and nutritious and can usually be boiled in the bag. If you are spending just a single night outdoors, consider freeze-dried food for your evening meal. It is probably worth the money for the high convenience factor.

■ MID-AFTERNOON By now you have probably been on your feet for at least six hours and energy levels will begin to take a dip. Coffee and rusks or biscuits (cookies) are great at raising flagging spirits, as are energy bars or chocolate, so refuel for the last leg of the journey.

■ SNACKS Snacking along the way is an excellent way to maintain your energy levels. Go for snacks high in energy, such as raisins, unsalted nuts, dried fruit, yoghurt bars, glucose sweets or Trail Mix. Easy-to-eat fruit, such as apples and bananas, work well as snacks too (but don't forget to take the peels home!). Concentrated energy drinks in powder form can be added to a water bottle to give an extra boost, especially in hot weather.

fluid per day should be ample replacement, but high temperatures combined with even a small amount of exercise may require you to take in more liquid. Remember that alcohol and caffeine both act as diuretics, speeding up the level of dehydration. If your urine becomes dark in colour and smells strongly, you need to start drinking with intent.

Hydration systems, incorporating bladder packs, drinking tubes and non-leak bite valves, enable you to drink on the move, thus effectively replacing the fluids your body loses while hiking. While perspiring, you also exude many salts and minerals. If you are hiking for more than four or five hours at a time, you should take an electrolytic solution to replace lost minerals.

Lastly, remember that on an overnight hike you will need water for personal hygiene and washing up, so factor this into your estimations.

Trail eating

A rule of thumb when hiking is to cater approximately 1kg (2 lb) of food per person per day, but you will know best what food your body needs to keep going. List when and what you eat during a regular day at home or at work and try to duplicate this in your trail menu.

Food needs to be lightweight, easy to carry, fun to eat, difficult to spoil, tasty and nutritious. This might sound like a long shot when you think of the trail food of old — oatmeal squares, tasteless soya mince and energy bars hard enough to knock out the teeth on a medium-sized grizzly. Fortunately outdoor retailers have responded to the demand of gourmet hikers and these days shelves are brimming with a harvest of scrumptious snacks and well-balanced meals. Don't forget herbs and spices; they weigh nearly nothing, but can change an average meal into a delightful feast.

Multi-day hikes

When you are planning on spending a few days or more in the outdoors, you need to step up the level of preparations during the various planning stages. Responsibility areas within the group should be listed (refer to pg 40), assigned to identified members during preliminary meetings and finally checked by the appointed group leader. Initial meetings should serve as discussion forums on where and when to go and then, once the required research on the route has been completed, final preparations can begin in earnest.

Preparations and planning
Places, permits and paperwork
Start by contacting the relevant authorities to obtain the necessary permission and permits. Places on many popular trails often have to be booked months in advance, particularly during peak holiday periods. Expect to pay a deposit, and a cancellation fee if you pull out at the last minute.

If you are planning a hike in another country, organizing the paperwork is probably best left to a reputable adventure-tour operator with direct access to the local authorities and who will be conversant with local customs and requirements. Nevertheless, if you are hiking in unfamiliar areas, never just assume that everything has been organized; check and double-check all the arrangements before departure and do some research of your own. There are fly-by-night operators who specialize in fleecing unsuspecting tourists, so investigate the credibility of your chosen operator by asking for references from previous customers.

Before departing on the hike, ensure all the relevant authorities are informed of your route, the details of your group, and an estimated time of return.

If you are travelling across borders, task a specific group member with travel arrangements such as visas, tickets, passports and travel insurance.

If you plan on visiting an out-of-the-way destination that lacks the normal tourism infrastructure, try contacting international travel or environmental organizations such as the World Wide Fund for Nature (WWF), the International Union for the Conservation of Nature and Natural Resources (IUCN) or the Youth Hostel Association first. Even if they are unable to help you, they should be able to put you in touch with the relevant parks departments, tourism associations, conservation agencies and government authorities.

above SOMETIMES JUST GETTING TO THE START OF A TRAIL CAN BE AN ADVENTURE IN ITSELF. MANY TRAVELLERS UNDERTAKE HIKES AS PART OF A LONGER TRIP TO A FOREIGN COUNTRY.

opposite YOUR FIRST AND LAST NIGHTS ARE OFTEN SPENT AT A HIKERS LODGE, ENABLING YOU TO MAKE AN EARLY START ON THE TRAIL, OR TO RELAX BEFORE YOUR JOURNEY HOME.

Emergencies and first aid

When out on a trail, a minor emergency can easily escalate, sometimes with serious consequences. It is therefore important that the group as a whole is informed of the necessary steps to take in case of any emergency: who should be contacted first, where satisfactory medical treatment may be received, whether any member of the group has a condition requiring specialized medication or treatment, and how to arrange a medical evacuation

Ensure that your first aid kit is adequately stocked for specific eventualities you might encounter en route. If you are travelling to a remote region, contact a travel clinic or global health organization regarding vaccination requirements and area-specific health risks. Pack pencil flares and a mirror for signalling and programme emergency contact numbers into your mobile phone (if you take one), making sure the phone is set up for international roaming if necessary.

Maps and navigation aids

Many popular hikes have route markers, directional signs and well-trodden paths to guide you along the way. On lesser-known trails however, you will need either the services of a reliable guide or a complete set of up-to-date topographical maps covering your intended route. Where possible, opt for both to forestall the very realistic likelihood of human error.

Maps can be acquired from the relevant government mapping or survey departments (preferably at a 1:50,000 scale). They should be laminated or stored in a waterproof, see-through holder. Checking the print date is important, as man-made landmarks, like roads, power lines or earth dams, may have been changed.

A well-written, up-to-date guidebook on the area will enable you to understand and appreciate local customs, history and tradition.

If you will be venturing off the beaten track, a compass, protractor, pencil and ruler are the bare necessities for traditional navigation and it is essential that you know how to use the compass.

Global Positioning System (GPS) units are affordable and user-friendly, making one a must-have on any serious trek. Your GPS can be pre-programmed with set co-ordinates for the route, thus simplifying navigation, but do make sure your maps are accurate. Google Earth and internet mapping software may also be utilized to research and map your route from anywhere in the world.

IN AN EMERGENCY, MANY DIFFERENT SKILLS MIGHT BE REQUIRED. IF YOU FIND YOURSELF IN A SITUATION THAT IS BEYOND YOUR CAPABILITIES, CALL FOR HELP RATHER THAN RISK MAKING THINGS WORSE.

Food

Just a couple of days on a trail can lead to a large appetite, so a well-planned daily menu is in order. Factor in at least two days' high-energy, emergency rations (in case you get lost) and don't be tempted to raid these until you are well and truly out of the woods. If you are travelling far afield, pre-purchase the bulk of your provisions before travelling to your destination as it is impossible to predict the availability of certain items. Special dietary requirements should be checked by your hike quartermaster. Also remember to pack cooking utensils, plus those handy little additions that make all the difference (think tinfoil, leak-proof containers, zip-lock bags, washing-up liquid, pot scourers, herbs, spices and cooking oil).

Water

The availability of potable water along the route will determine your liquid assets when you set off. Play it safe, stocking up with enough water to last 24 hours beyond your expected date of replenishment. Purification tablets and a reputable filter pump are non-negotiable, as even the most dependable water source might have a dead creature drifting in it. If you are unsure of your water purifier's efficiency, first boil the water for at least 10 minutes and then use it in conjunction with water-purification tablets. (If you add the tablets before filtering, the purifier will remove any chemical taste from the water, leaving it both pleasant-tasting and safe to drink.)

Weather forecast

With the advent of the internet, accessing dependable weather information is an easy task, but it would be wise to compare information from various sites. A capable local guide with the requisite outdoor knowledge will often be able to anticipate changes in the weather, enabling you to take the necessary precautions well in advance.

Clothing

Pack comfortable clothing covering all eventualities, using rainfall figures and the mean minimum and

USE A WATER FILTER AND PURIFICATION TABLETS AT ALL TIMES, UNLESS YOU ARE 100 PER CENT CERTAIN THE WATER IS SAFE TO DRINK.

maximum temperatures in an area as a guideline. Useful hints are: you can never have too many pairs of good socks, a decent raincoat weighs next to nothing, a pair of comfortable, dry shoes will rejuvenate tired feet, and you lose most of your heat through your head. Keep in mind that extreme climates require technical garments with a tried and tested track record. When it comes to clothing, rather err on the side of caution than be caught short in bad weather.

Other gear

Double-check all those little items that tend to slip through the woodwork: there is simply no excuse for forgetting your sunglasses, a hat, a 10m (30ft) section of strong rope, waterproof matches or a lighter, a whistle, toilet paper and sun-protection lotion. Don't forget to include a field guide for the area.

If you are planning a hike that requires specialist gear, make sure you are fully conversant in the use of such equipment. Venturing into an extreme situation without the necessary equipment and skills not only endangers your own life, but also puts at risk any rescue personnel who may have to bail you out under emergency conditions.

On a multi-day hike you can expect to carry anything from 12–30kg (26–65 lb), or more in extreme cases. It will therefore be necessary to distribute weight as evenly as possible, placing regularly used kit in easily accessible locations such as side, top or belt pockets or in the shock-cord carry system.

The concept of load-sharing will bring about savings in both weight and space. You probably need only one each of items such as a first aid kit, flares, spade, rope, lantern and a stove and these, as well as individual sections of the tents, may be shared out between group members. (Use the kit check list on page 93 as a handy guide when packing).

With the exception of those items constantly required, separate your load into food; cooking utensils, cutlery and crockery; lanterns, candles, batteries and fuel; sleeping bags; toiletries; clean and dirty clothing; safety and first aid equipment; compass, GPS and maps, camera, MP3 player and other electronic equipment.

Pack these groups separately, possibly in colour-coded plastic bags or stuff sacks for easy identification when rummaging around your pack. This will keep smells from migrating, make it easier to locate specific items and prevent leaking cooking fuel, for example, from messing up everything in your pack.

Try to limit your pack's weight to between 20 per cent and one third of your body weight, correlating carry-weight to your personal levels of strength and fitness. Also remember to waterproof your pack by lining its compartments with garbage bags or bin liners.

■ **LOWER MAIN COMPARTMENT**
Traditionally reserved for your sleeping bag, but size and weight step-downs now leave additional space (except in the case of extreme cold weather bags).

Stash extra footwear, thermal fleece or a raincoat (if you don't expect to need them in a hurry), sleeping bag-liner or inner sheet, and splash cover for your pack here. Anything breakable can be wrapped in your sleeping bag for added protection.

■ **UPPER MAIN COMPARTMENT**
Food, cooking utensils, flares, lantern and fuel, and clothing can go in here. Distribute the weight and place the food and gear required for the day close to the top. Include safety equipment, sun protection and a personal first aid kit if you can.

In many packs, the division between the top and bottom compartments can be unzipped to allow tall items (such as collapsible fishing rods, rolled up maps or camera monopods) to be conveniently packed.

■ **BELT POCKET** Small zipped pockets on the hip belt are perfect for on-the-go access to essentials such as lip salve, sun block, tissues, energy bars or sweets, spare film, money, sunglasses or similar.

■ **LOWER SIDE POCKETS** Pack snacks and drink mixes, plus any food required for the day, into a side pocket, so that it is easily accessible without taking the pack off. If you are not using a hydration system (see below), then use one side pocket to stash your water bottle, or a small stove and the makings for a hot drink along the way.

■ **TOP SIDE POCKETS** A small mess kit, including a mug, cutlery, multi-tool and washing-up items should fit into one pocket (muffle with socks or a scarf to prevent distracting rattles). Use the other pocket for your personal toiletries, a hat, cap or Balaclava, insect repellent, hand or head torch and a whistle.

■ **TOP POCKET** Backpacks are often designed to allow this section to be detachable for use as a bumbag or hip pack. Use it

to store fragile equipment and items you need to access easily. It is a perfect spot for your compass, GPS, maps and other navigation items, guidebooks, trail permits, travel documents, binoculars and camera.

■ **SHOCK-CORD CARRYING SYSTEM** Use the elastic grid to secure clothes that need to dry out before they go back into the pack.

■ **BOTTOM EQUIPMENT STRAPS** Use these to secure your tent, foam sleeping mat or water containers, as well as specialist tools like crampons and ice axes.

■ **HIKING POLE POCKETS** Designed for safely storing your hiking poles.

■ **SPLASH COVER** If it looks like rain, make sure this is accessible before you start out.

■ **HYDRATION SYSTEM SLEEVE** Many contemporary backpack designs now feature either an internal or external bladder sleeve, thus allowing effective water storage and easy replenishment. Additional

water may be kept in squeeze bottles in the side pockets, or in a lightweight, insulated storage bladder secured to the outside of your pack. Ensure that all containers are fully sealed, because you don't want to run out of water or find your water supply inconveniently decanted into the contents of your pack.

Following the trail

If there is one factor upon which the success of a multi-day hike rests, it is communication. The responsibility for keeping the party together rests squarely on the shoulders of the appointed group leader, who must make sure that constant visual and aural contact is maintained between all members. The leader will keep an eye on slower members, letting them set the pace and assisting them wherever possible. On some hiking routes there are no easily discernible tracks or route markers and, in some cases, you will be traversing a mountain range or wilderness area. Be especially alert in dense vegetation, on undulating or broken terrain or when visibility is diminished due to mist, rain, smoke or approaching nightfall, as it is easy for the group to become separated under these conditions.

Most hiking routes are divided into daily sections varying in distance and degree of difficulty and you have to regulate your hiking speed in order to reach the designated camping areas or huts by nightfall.

Maintaining a constant pace is easy enough along firm, flat sections of a trail, but is complicated by variations in terrain. It is therefore necessary to study the map before setting off in order to evaluate the terrain you will encounter along the way. This will allow you to plan regular stops based on time spent along the route rather than actual distance travelled. For example, an easy walk along a valley floor might see you cover 5km (3 miles) in an hour, while on a steep, rocky climb out of the valley your speed of advance could drop to less than 2km (1 mile) per hour.

When you move off a discernible trail, you might slow down even more as you have to navigate along a compass bearing. A good idea is to find out the local sunset time and use it to calculate the duration required for various legs and stops along the route.

IN MISTY OR OVERCAST CONDITIONS, IT IS IMPERATIVE FOR MEMBERS OF THE GROUP TO REMAIN WITHIN SIGHT OF ONE ANOTHER.

When carrying a heavy backpack, correct posture is imperative to avoid back pain or even spinal damage. This can be achieved through correctly packing and distributing the load on your back. Too much weight on your shoulders will force them backwards, thus arching your spine and leading to upper body fatigue and possible spinal problems.

If you are carrying an excessively heavy pack, fit the harness while sitting and ask a hiking partner to help you stand up. With a lighter, more manageable pack, just slip your stronger arm through the shoulder harness and swing the pack onto your back in one smooth movement.

Tighten the hip belt around your waist, keeping the weight mainly on your hips. Adjust the weight on your shoulders by using the load-lifter tabs on the shoulder harness to vary the vertical positioning of the pack on your back. Making adjustments while you walk helps to reduce fatigue in both your lower back and upper body by distributing the pack load between these areas. Although snug, the hip belt should not restrict your movements or be too tight around the stomach (look for a rounded, ergonomic design, with broad webbing and ample padding).

A chest (sternum) strap, linking the two shoulder straps across your upper chest, will further stabilize the pack on your back by keeping the shoulder harness together, thus keeping the pack flush against your body, not pulling away from it.

Make sure the size and length of your pack corresponds to your body height, as this enhances the overall fit. Optimize the pack's position on your back by using the vertical adjustment strap to adjust the position of the vertical harness.

IF YOU ARE CARRYING A HEAVY PACK, FIT THE HARNESS WHILE SITTING AND ASK A HIKING PARTNER TO HELP YOU STAND UPRIGHT.

A BADLY ADJUSTED PACK THAT FORCES YOU TO COMPENSATE BY LEANING TOO FAR BACKWARDS CAN CAUSE SPINAL PROBLEMS.

LIT BY THE GLOW OF A LANTERN, A DOME TENT PITCHED FOR THE NIGHT IN WYOMING'S BIG HORN MOUNTAINS, PROVIDES A SENSE OF HOME.

Setting up camp

If you are not stopping at a designated place, don't leave site selection too late; there is nothing worse than ending up camping in an exposed, uncomfortable position because you ran out of daylight.

If there are no specified camping sites along the route, study your map before you set off in the morning, identifying a few possible sites where you might spend the night. The bigger the distance between the topographical (contour) lines on the map, the flatter the area will be.

For many hikers, proximity to water equates to a good camping site. This is not only because of the obvious availability of water for cooking, washing and swimming, but also because being near water often provides a profound sense of tranquillity.

A whole range of factors come into play when deciding on where to camp though, so look beyond obvious scenic beauty.

For example, a camp site located near a swamp might expose you to constant insect activity; or you could counter humidity by opting for a site higher up a slope where a night breeze will keep you cool.

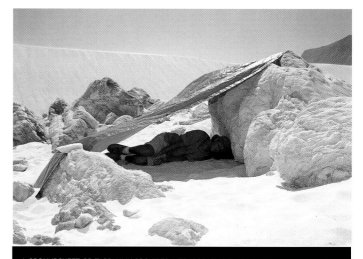

A GROUNDSHEET OR TARPAULIN PROVIDES A TEMPORARY REFUGE FROM THE MIDDAY SUN. IT CAN ALSO MAKE A BASIC SHELTER IN AN EMERGENCY, BUT OFFERS LIMITED PROTECTION.

Identifying a suitable camp site

Your first consideration should be safety. Study the area to ensure that you are well clear of precariously perched rocks or potentially rotten tree branches, that you are above the high-water mark of rivers, outside canyons or kloofs where you might be trapped by flash floods, and out of the path of avalanches. High-water levels may be determined by looking for debris, usually a line of dry plant matter, along the river or canyon side.

If you are in an area where dangerous animals roam, make sure you are not intruding on their home range. Inspect caves or overhangs for signs of habitation. Sleeping burrows, loose hair, droppings, tracks, meal remains and strong smells are all very real pointers to habitation. Carefully check trails to and from any water for tracks. These might be access routes for large animals coming to drink or leaving the water to graze, so position yourself well off to the side where you will be out of danger.

Try to determine from which direction the prevailing wind blows and set up camp in the lee of a rocky outcrop or a dense stand of trees or other vegetation, thus ensuring relative protection from the elements.

If you expect an electrical storm with lightning, play it safe by moving away from exposed high ground and obvious lightning conductors such as tall trees or electricity pylons, opting for a dry cave, rock overhang or low stands of bush instead.

In a desert you might have to rest during the hottest part of the day, so do your best to locate a tree or high rocks for shade. (An alternative would be to create a patch of shade with your fly sheet and hiking poles.)

Lastly, make sure you don't pick the one spot frequented by everyone else — the last thing you want is a noisy bunch arriving as you're settling down to enjoy a peaceful sunset.

IN AREAS WHERE INSECTS ARE PROLIFIC, YOU MAY SPEND MOST OF YOUR TIME UNDER COVER, AND A LIGHTWEIGHT MOSQUITO NET MAY BE COOLER THAN A TENT.

Once you find that perfect site, you need to allocate four basic usage areas: the sleeping quarters where you will pitch your tent; a kitchen area where you will be making a fire (if one is allowed) and preparing meals; a washing area for cleaning yourself as well as doing the dishes and any laundry; and an ablution section to disappear to when nature calls.

■ **THE BEDROOM (A)** First identify the right spot in which to pitch your tent. Drainage should be good so that if it rains, water won't be channelled towards your tent or pool around it.

It is important to find a flat, level pitching area, otherwise you'll spend most of the night migrating towards the down slope side of the tent before crawling back up again. If you do find a spot with soft grass or fine sand, rest assured in the knowledge that the benevolent gods of camping are smiling upon you.

Pitch the tent with its opening facing away from inclement weather, anchoring it well with tent pegs or stones to make sure a sudden storm cannot flatten it during the night. This also applies to free-standing tents, especially in high wind areas.

When venturing into areas where heavy snowfalls occur, invest in a four-season tent and be aware of potential avalanches.

Keep your tent at least 100m (110yd) away from the water source and the toilet area and far enough from other tents to allow a decent sense of privacy.

■ **THE KITCHEN (B)** If fires are allowed, first prize is a flat, sandy patch between some rocks which can shield the flames from the wind. Be careful of making a fire on bedrock, as the upper layers of stone may expand and crack due to the heat, causing a series of explosions which will

THE IDEAL CAMP SITE MAY SEEM IMPOSSIBLE TO FIND BUT, WITH AN UNDERSTANDING OF THE BASIC USAGE AREAS, IT IS POSSIBLE TO ADAPT ANY LOCATION TO SUIT YOUR PURPOSES. ALWAYS TAKE ACCOUNT OF REGULATIONS PERTAINING TO THE ROUTE, AND OBSERVE RULES SUCH AS WHERE TO BUILD A FIRE OR POSITION THE ABLUTION AREA. RESPECT FOR NATURE AND COURTESY TOWARDS FELLOW HIKERS ARE SIMPLE PRINCIPLES TO UPHOLD.

scatter coals all over the place. Avoid having a fire too close to your tent for exactly this reason, as even sparks can burn holes in your fly sheet.

If there is no obvious place to make a fire, dig a trench about 80cm long by 40cm wide and 30cm deep (30 x 16 x 12in), thus sinking your fire into the ground.

In extremely wet conditions, it may be necessary to use your stove inside the porch area of your tent, but do make sure that it is stable and can't tip over.

Your outside kitchen site can also double as a storage area. Anything that cannot be stored inside your tent or its awnings should be kept well away from the unwanted attention of night-time prowlers, both human and animal. Food should be securely packed and suspended from a high tree branch to discourage animals from snacking on your provisions during the night.

Strong, sealable containers, called bear barrels, will keep tempting smells in while keeping ants, insects and animals out.

■ **THE BATHROOM (C)** Look for a grassy, secluded spot, but remember to keep at least 100m (110yd) between you and the nearest water source, as even biodegradable soap could affect the delicate balance of an aquatic ecosystem. If you decide

A SOFT GRASSY PATCH WITH A VIEW OF THE WATER, A WARM SUNNY EVENING AND THE COMPANY OF FRIENDS - WHAT MORE COULD ONE ASK FOR AT THE END OF A DAY'S HIKING?

to carry a solar bag shower, find a suitable tree from which to hang it (if possible, in direct sunlight to warm the water), otherwise do your thing with a cup and bucket.

On hikes where there is a shortage of water, it might be necessary to re-use bath water in order to do dishes or laundry.

■ **THE LATRINE (D)** Try to locate this out of view of other campers, for decency's sake, but ideally, with a panoramic view across the landscape. The soil should be soft enough to dig a 15–30cm (6–12in) hole, thus keeping excrement within the

biological disposal layer. In a heavy-usage area, devise some way of marking used spots, possibly by planting a stick in the ground, to prevent fellow hikers from unearthing your valued contributions.

At all times, set up your camp site in such a way that you minimize your impact on the environment. Don't break off branches or roll logs or rocks around, or make fires if they are not permitted. Before you move on, tamp down furrows, remove all your garbage, fill in fire trenches and try to leave the area the way you found it.

Specialist skills & activities

there is a lot more to hiking than just putting one foot in front of the other and admiring the view as you go. Even within an individual country, the climate, terrain and natural environment can vary from region to region, and dedicated hikers may find themselves venturing into totally unfamiliar conditions as they move further afield to explore new trails and expand their hiking repertoire.

In an alien environment, unprepared hikers can quickly find themselves in difficulty, so it is prudent to learn some advanced skills before venturing into areas where you may encounter potential dangers. Enlist the services of a trained guide or experienced hiker until you are confident in your own abilities and remember, when in doubt, rather turn back than regret it later.

Various specialist techniques have been perfected to help hikers adapt to diverse terrain and obstacles. Some of these activities, especially those crossing over into the realm of mountaineering, have long since developed into disciplines in their own right. Abseiling (rappelling), canyoneering and traversing are examples of skills you might find indispensable on a technically demanding hike, but sometimes even an undemanding route can suddenly throw up an unexpected challenge that requires a cool head and a knowledge of some advanced skills and techniques.

above THE WEATHERED SANDSTONE RIDGES OF A DESERT CANYON DWARF A PAIR OF HIKERS SILHOUETTED AGAINST THE SKY.

opposite WALKING ACROSS HARD-PACKED ICE AND SNOW REQUIRES CRAMPONS AND AN ICE AXE, AS WELL AS A GOOD SENSE OF BALANCE.

While proper research beforehand should have prepared you for the expected conditions on your hike, there is always the possibility that nature will be having an off-day; or you may get lost and find yourself facing a situation you were not expecting. Tackling different terrain is easier when you are trained and properly equipped, so if there is the possibility of encountering obstacles such as snow, ice or steep cliffs, make sure you are prepared in advance.

■ **SCREE SLOPES** The definition of a scree slope is a 'sloping mass of rocks at the base of a cliff'. Usually formed through extreme expansion and contraction erosion, these rock segments are sharp, slippery and unstable, making them very unsafe to negotiate. When crossing scree slopes, use hiking poles for additional balance and stability, or scramble along on all fours. Make sure of every move, checking your footing with each step. A short stay rope, controlled by someone from a secure area, can be used to anchor members as they move across a scree slope.

■ **DESERTS AND DUNES** The shortest route is rarely the fastest when walking on sand. Rather scout for firm sand and stick to that, shortening your strides to lessen impact and to generate constant forward momentum. Nothing causes blisters more quickly than sand in your shoes, so avoid this by taping up your socks or wearing gaiters, especially when striding or sliding down soft dune sand.

■ **CLIFFS** Ascending (scaling or jumaring) or descending a cliff should only be attempted if someone in your party has the necessary rock climbing experience and the proper equipment. A belay rope, friction devices and a harness will ensure that, if you do lose your handhold during an ascent, the distance of your fall is minimized and

effectively checked. The technique employed when descending a vertical cliff is called abseiling (rappelling) and involves being strapped into a harness and attached to a rope via a friction device with which you control your rate of descent. Double-check all knots and anchor points and make sure you have enough rope to reach the bottom of the cliff.

■ **SNOW** While snow might add a dimension of tranquillity to your surroundings, it makes hiking difficult, as the trail can quickly become invisible, necessitating navigation, while simultaneously making walking more tentative. Set a course according to identifiable topographical features, signs or tracks left by other walkers or trail builders, or along obvious lines of advance. Where possible, stick to hard-packed snow to avoid expending energy by constantly sinking in up to your thighs. Hiking poles are useful to help gauge the depth of the snow and give you something to

lean on in unstable terrain. If you expect to encounter large amounts of snow on the hike, or hike regularly in winter, it may be worth investing in snowshoes or cross-country skis.

■ **ICE** Walking over hard ice is an art form in itself and a sense of balance and the right gear will stand you in good stead. Don't even think of taking on ice without an ice axe and crampons (and make sure you know how to use them). Crampons strap to the soles of your boots and add a handy set of spikes to your feet. They are perfect for digging in when crossing patches of ice or while ascending a frozen slope. Use the ice axe as an insurance policy when you slip, by embedding the long, narrow pick in the ice and hanging on to the handle to arrest your slide (make sure you have the loop around your wrist). The square-shaped adze (cutting tool) on the other end of the ice axe may be used to carve out steps when moving up a steep ice or snow slope.

Specialist activities

Once you have mastered the basics and conquered a few trails, you may want to seek out new challenges or expand your range of skills. This section touches briefly on some specialist activities, conveying a concise overview of the theory, technique and gear involved. Please note that these descriptions merely serve as an introduction. It is essential to invest in proper training, or enlist the service of qualified guides before you undertake these activities. Your life could be at stake.

Canyoneering

Canyoneering refers to hiking through, into or across a canyon, ravine or crevasse. Also known as canyoning or kloofing, canyoneering is an adventure activity that combines mountaineering and hiking skills, including boulder-hopping, wading, scrambling, rock climbing and abseiling (rappelling). A primary danger when canyoneering is getting caught in a flash flood, so before you depart, ascertain the extent of the watershed and check recent and future weather forecasts for reports of heavy rains. As you progress, be aware of any changes in the water level and identify possible escape routes from the canyon.

Technique   Expect to swim and wade through icy water, negotiate rapids and waterfalls, jump off cliffs into deep pools, abseil down canyon walls, scramble or climb along steep cliffs and jump from rock to rock across gaping chasms.

Walking, wading and boulder-hopping are slippery activities, so use your hands or trekking poles to maintain balance. Ensure that your pack is waterproofed and easy to unclip if you slip into deep water.

When jumping into pools, always check the depth of the water and scan below the surface for evidence of submerged rocks, logs or other obstacles which could injure you. Try to land at a slight backwards angle, entering feet first and immediately kicking out and spreading your arms to halt your descent.

Negotiating rapids requires its own set of skills: wear a PFD (personal flotation device) and float down in a seated position with your feet forward, using your legs and buttocks to absorb any impacts.

Only attempt technical climbing (using a rope) if you have the proper equipment and someone in the group is experienced in setting up the ropes and anchors for belaying or abseiling (rappelling).

Gear and equipment   One good tip when canyoneering is to wear a wet suit, as this will protect you against minor knocks and scratches, keep you warm and give you extra buoyancy during deep water crossings. Don't forget to pack a length of rope, slings, carabiners, a climbing harness and a helmet. A PFD will not only help you float, but will also cushion you during jumps and while negotiating river rapids.

Footwear choices vary from river sandals and aqua shoes to scuba booties; look for quick-drying materials, high-grip rubber soles and a lightweight construction. Hypothermia is a very real possibility, so keep an extra set of clothing in a waterproof bag and carry a shell jacket to protect you against the wind chill.

CANYONS ARE POTENTIAL HAZARDS, AS AN UNEXPECTED FLASH FLOOD CAN TRAP YOU IN RAGING WATERS. ALWAYS ENSURE YOU HAVE THE MEANS AND SKILL TO MAKE A RAPID EXIT IF NECESSARY.

WHEN EXPLORING SECTIONS OF COASTLINE, PROTECTIVE HEADGEAR AND A PFD ARE ESSENTIAL AND A WET SUIT IS PREFERABLE IN COLD WATER.

Coasteering

This is an activity very similar to canyoneering, except that you will be traversing the coastline rather than a river course. You will still be rock-hopping, climbing and hiking, but in a marine environment, with the added element of danger. The action of waves, tides and currents, circumventing or crossing estuaries and lagoons, and slogging along beaches and over sand dunes are added to your list of possible obstacles.

The constantly varying water levels along the coast are a risk and should be monitored at all times. Use printed tide tables to predict high or low (ebb) tides and neap or spring tides (the phases of the moon may help with the latter). Watch out for freak waves and be mindful of riptides and hidden currents when passing through estuaries. Sharks often feed in estuaries or where rivers flow into the sea, so where possible, cross the river higher up or use a boat.

Technique Walking is easiest along the firmest part of the beach, so try to stick to the sand immediately above the water mark. When an occasional cliff jump or stretch of rock-hopping is required, keep an eye on wave activity. Remember that waves advance in sets of seven, so judge your jumps to coincide with the ebb and flow of the water. Be especially cautious of seaweed, as tangling in long and tough kelp strands could easily lead to trouble. If you are swept away by a current, do not fight against it, but rather attempt to swim perpendicular to the flow until you escape its force, then make your way back to the shore.

Gear and equipment A waterproof pack and warm clothing is essential and, as in canyoneering, it helps to wear a wet suit when in the water. Always use a PFD to help you cope with swells and the tide; keep a diving knife accessible in case you get caught in kelp and use trekking poles to maintain your footing along a slippery tidal shelf. This is where good shoes are important. You need rugged, non-slip soles to cope with mussel beds and sharp rocks, while cushioning will be essential to cope with beach runs and boulder hopping. Tight neoprene ankle cuffs will keep sand and debris out of your shoes, while quick-draining uppers will help your feet to dry out quickly. Guard against hypothermia with a spare set of dry clothes and a windproof shell.

WHEN WALKING ALONG A RIDGE, KEEP WELL BACK FROM THE CREST AS THE SNOW MAY BE WEAK AND COULD COLLAPSE, WITH DIRE CONSEQUENCES.

High-altitude hiking

Even in tropical or arid countries, high-altitude routes, those above 4000m (13,000ft), usually go hand in hand with severe cold, ice and at least some snow. In such extreme environments, poor judgement may quickly lead to injury, or even death. Assessing the structure of an ice obstacle, the stability of a snow slope or the probability of an avalanche occurring are intuitive skills that should be entrusted to experienced mountaineers where possible. Despite the apparent harshness of high-altitude environments, always remember that mountain ecosystems are extremely sensitive to damage and pollution.

Techniques When traversing snow and ice, even basic functions such as walking need to be re-learned. Some skills to master before you head for the heights include glissading (sliding down a snow slope on your buttocks), climbing (including snow and ice belays), walking with crampons, the use of ice axes, surviving an avalanche, ascending steep terrain by kicking steps, and constructing snow holes to shelter the group.

Gear and equipment One cannot stress enough the importance of the correct choice of equipment when embarking on a high-altitude hike, but it will be of no value if you don't know how to use it. In blizzard conditions, not even the most expensive tent can save you if you are unable to pitch it effectively. The same goes for all camping, cooking and other technical equipment, so thoroughly familiarize yourself with how they work before setting off. Footwear and clothing should also be specifically designed for the climate extremes you will encounter along the way.

Mountaineering

Often a hill-walking section along a trail will suddenly morph into a craggy rock slope, leaving you faced with one of two options; either scouting about for another route or knuckling down and scrambling upwards. If you have the experience and equipment, the occasional climb or rock scramble could save you a lot of time, simultaneously adding to an immediate gain in elevation. Keep in mind though, that mountaineering, or climbing, is an extremely unforgiving sport and any miscalculation or lapse in judgement may have extreme consequences.

Techniques Mountaineering covers an extensive and variable set of skills, taking in a wide range of technical disciplines, including scrambling, jumaring, free-climbing, high-line or Tyrolean traverses, bouldering and abseiling (rappelling). None of these activities should be attempted without proper training and the right equipment. Contact a local climbing club for information on basic mountaineering and abseiling courses.

Gear and equipment Rugged clothing and footwear are required when moving into craggy mountain territory. High altitudes are usually synonymous with low temperatures, so opt for dual purpose, waterproof footwear that can handle both walking and scrambling, as well as technical clothing designed to cope with extreme temperatures.

Mandatory safety equipment includes an approved protective helmet and well-fitting climbing harness, plus a sufficient length of good climbing rope, carabiners and a range of friction devices and the knowledge of how to use them. There is no substitute for proper training when it comes to climbing mountains.

above ABSEILING IS A QUICK WAY TO GET OFF A CLIFF, PROVIDED YOU HAVE THE SKILLS.

top SCALING A ROCKY RIDGE MAY LOOK EASY FROM ONE SIDE, BUT BEFORE YOU LEAD YOUR GROUP INTO UNFORESEEN DANGER, MAKE SURE YOU CAN DESCEND JUST AS EASILY.

Animal tracking

Observing animals in their natural habitat adds an exciting dimension to a walk on the wild side, but could lead to potentially dangerous situations. When you are accompanied by an armed guard or ranger (as on organized primate tracking excursions or hikes in wilderness reserves and national parks), these officials will determine and guide your actions. Pay attention during pre-walk briefings, as the regulations are aimed at protecting both you and the animals during close encounters. Many wilderness areas around the world do not insist on guides, leaving you to face potentially dangerous wildlife on your own.

All large animals should be given a wide berth. Keep your eyes open for signs and tracks and, if you do happen upon wild beasts unexpectedly, maintain visual contact while slowly retreating to safety. Once you're out of sight, move downwind so that the animals are unable to pick up your scent. Always enquire about potential dangers before setting out and, where possible, opt to be accompanied by a reputable guide.

Hiking with dogs

Many trail organizations allow dogs along sections of their routes that fall outside of national parks, game reserves or protected natural areas.

Having a dog on the trail does bring with it many responsibilities, the first of which is to make sure that your canine companion subscribes to trail etiquette in the same way as humans would. Damaging vegetation, chasing animals, stealing food, loud barking, aggressive behaviour, setting dog-doo land mines and other furry faux pas are cause enough to antagonize even the most peaceful of dog lovers.

Dogs are easy to pack for: all they need is a recommended daily serving of a balanced, nutritionally tested dry food plus enough water to keep their tails wagging. Specially designed dog-packs even enable them to carry their own rations! Your dog should be at least one year old (otherwise bone damage might occur), but still young and energetic enough to cope with the longest walkies it will ever have in its life. If in any doubt, consult your vet beforehand.

A RANGER OR GUIDE WILL HAVE A WEALTH OF KNOWLEDGE ABOUT THE PLANT AND ANIMAL LIFE ALONG THE TRAIL, ENABLING YOU TO LEARN ABOUT THE ECOLOGY OF A SPECIFIC ENVIRONMENT AND THE CONTRIBUTION THAT EACH ELEMENT MAKES TO THE FUNCTIONING OF THE WHOLE.

ALL KITTED OUT AND READY TO GO! PROVIDED DOGS ARE WELL-TRAINED, OBEDIENT AND WILL NOT STRAY, HIKING WITH CANINE COMPANIONS ENHANCES THE ALREADY STRONG BOND BETWEEN MAN AND HIS BEST FRIEND. ENSURE THOUGH, THAT YOUR ANIMALS ARE WELCOME ON THE TRAIL.

Hiking with disabilities

THE JOËLETTE™ IS A SPECIALLY-DESIGNED WHEELCHAIR THAT PERMITS DISABLED PEOPLE TO UNDERTAKE SIMPLE HIKES WITH THE ASSISTANCE OF ABLE-BODIED COMPANIONS.

Having a physical disability need not preclude you from appreciating the great outdoors. Many trail operators and commercial hiking organizations offer a range of accessible trails in different environments for people with varying degrees and types of disability. Know your own limitations and enquire beforehand as to the facilities and services offered so that you and your hiking companions are well-prepared and properly equipped.

Navigation and first aid

Once you step into the arena of multi-day hiking excursions, you will find the need for self reliance intensifying as the distance between you and civilization increases. In developed countries, you may make it to the nearest town to arrange a medical evacuation if something goes wrong. However, destinations in countries with less-developed infrastructures might require you to cope with medical and other emergencies by relying largely on your own skills and equipment.

Conventional navigation skills are essential if you will be venturing into countries where a general lack of resources, and unsophisticated communications networks, can make electronic navigation difficult.

Navigation techniques

Wander around in the wilderness for long enough and you are bound to lose your way. Often you will be able to re-trace your footsteps, recognize a landmark or ask for directions, but at other times skilful navigation and orienteering will be required to get you back on track. Join an orienteering club or attend a navigational skills clinic to brush up on your abilities before setting off into the wilds.

How to find your way

There are many ways of orienting yourself without the assistance of navigational aids. First, try to establish where north is, which is relatively easy once you know

above ESTABLISHING YOUR POSITION BY USING A MAP IS A FUNDAMENTAL SKILL TO BE MASTERED BY ANYONE HEADING FOR THE GREAT OUTDOORS.

opposite EMERGENCY EVACUATION IS A WORST-CASE SCENARIO, BUT WHEN A LIFE IS AT STAKE, CALLING FOR HELP MAY BE THE BEST OPTION.

where the sun and moon rise (roughly east) and set (roughly west). As you move further away from the equator, you will also be able to determine north and south by the sun's position at midday. In the northern hemisphere the sun will be due south at noon; in the southern hemisphere, the sun will be due north at its noon point (the direction in which flowers face is another good indication).

North and south may also be determined by using the night sky. In the northern hemisphere, identify the North (or Pole) Star; it lies at the axis of the earth's rotation and therefore holds a constant position due north. Locate the star by establishing the position of the Big Dipper and the Milky Way (see diagram A).

The Southern Cross will help you orient yourself when south of the equator. Draw an imaginary line through the longer axis of the cross and another line at right angles to a line drawn between the two pointers. Extend these imaginary lines until they meet and, from this point, take a line straight down to the horizon to determine true south. (See diagram B below).

Natural phenomena you can use to find your way are rivers (check their direction of flow), the prevailing wind direction (look at the shape of trees, bushes or dunes) and moss or lichen growing on the shaded side of trees or rocks (on the south side in the southern hemisphere, north side in the northern hemisphere).

Once you are able to orient yourself directionally, you can begin to compare landmarks and natural features on a map with your immediate surroundings, thus positioning yourself. When moving through dense vegetation, mark your trail as you progress, but do so without damaging the environment; instead of slashing tree trunks or breaking branches, pack small stones into cairns or arrows tracing your direction.

Map information

Although map indexing systems, symbols (map legend) and references vary from country to country, basic markings remain the same, thus allowing you to interpret most maps to orient yourself.

Latitudinal lines (east to west) are measured in degrees, minutes and seconds from the equator, which lies at zero degrees. Longitudinal lines (north to south), are divided in the same way, with the Greenwich meridian (zero degrees) running through the UK, and longitude denoted in degrees east or west of this line. The International Date Line lies opposite the Greenwich meridian, at 180 degrees.

Contour lines and the intervals between them depict the elevation of natural features on the map and vary depending on the scale (usually a 50m/165ft interval at a scale of 1:250 000). Hypsometric tints (the use of colours) may also graphically indicate elevation.

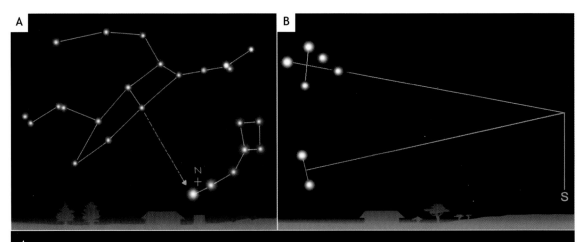

A THE NORTH STAR HOLDS A CONSTANT POSITION ROUGHLY ABOVE THE NORTH POLE AND CAN BE LOCATED BY ITS PROXIMITY TO THE BIG DIPPER.

B THE SOUTHERN CROSS IS THE KEY TO ESTABLISHING SOUTH IN THE SOUTHERN HEMISPHERE, BUT DOES NOT HOLD A CONSTANT POSITION.

A legend (explanation) at the bottom of the sheet contains a key to the symbols used for mapping both natural and man-made features. It also indicates the scale (degree of reduction) of the map, the map number, its relation to adjoining maps and the date of printing.

Knowing when a map was printed is important, as the older the map, the more changes there may be between the man-made structures, such as roads, dams and power lines, indicated on the map and the actual situation on the ground.

Lastly, look for the magnetic declination, a graphic diagram indicating the difference between true and magnetic north for a specific location. This figure, shown in degrees and minutes, will indicate an angle to be added or subtracted to your compass reading in order to establish a true north reading.

New technology

Wearable computers combine the functions of a compass, altimeter, barometer, watch and heart-rate monitor into a package the size of a chunky wristwatch. This simplifies many navigational issues on the trail by not only giving you directional bearings, but also your altitude above sea level. In addition, barometric pressure readings enable you to predict changes in the weather (at least to some extent).

Global Positioning System (GPS) receivers use permanently positioned satellites orbiting the earth to plot your exact position through triangulation, and are usually accurate to within a few metres (or feet). A hand-held GPS allows you to capture way-points along the route, enabling you to re-trace your steps, or even to plot a course before you set off, using a series of pre-determined coordinates.

Remember to always have a an alternative plan in place, as electronic devices (and especially their power sources) can easily fail, particularly in adverse weather – just when you need them the most.

above A COMPASS, TOPOGRAPHICAL MAP AND A GPS DEVICE ARE HIGHLY EFFECTIVE WHEN USED IN CONJUNCTION WITH EACH OTHER.

top IF YOU KNOW THE PREVAILING WIND DIRECTION IN AN AREA, THE SHAPE OF WIND-FORMED TREES WILL HELP YOU TO ESTABLISH THE COMPASS POINTS.

centre MAP READING SKILLS AND THE ABILITY TO ORIENTATE YOURSELF ARE ESSENTIAL IF YOU WANT TO HIKE OFF THE BEATEN TRACK.

Orientation (locating your position within the landscape) and navigation (moving along a known bearing through the landscape) are simplified when you have the right equipment. In addition to a topographical map, you need a compass, a protractor, a sharp pencil and a ruler. Other handy items are a distance roller (to calculate distances along squiggly lines) and a hand-held GPS (Global Positioning System). The basic steps of orienting yourself and plotting a route are as follows:

■ Start the process of orienting your map by aligning it with the surrounding terrain. Compare features such as rivers, valleys, hills, mountains, roads or power lines and match the map to these (1).

■ To get precise alignment to true north, adjust the compass for magnetic declination by rotating the bezel or compass housing, 'offsetting' the orienting arrow by the magnetic declination given on the map (2). Then align the compass base plate with the side of the map (or the North/South grid lines) and turn both the map and compass until the needle aligns with the orienting arrow in the compass housing.

The map is now aligned to true north (3).

■ In order to plot your route, you first need to establish exactly where you are on the map. To do this, you need to triangulate your position by taking an initial bearing on a recognizable landmark and then drawing a line from it through and beyond your estimated position (4).

Repeat with a second landmark at an angle of at least 45 degrees away from the first landmark, indicating the compass bearing on the map with a pencil line (5).

Your present position on the map will be where the two lines cross. You can verify this by taking a third bearing, which should bisect the intersection of the first two lines.

■ Now that you know where you are, you need to plot a course to your destination. Study the map and the terrain around you, as the shortest route will not necessarily be the quickest. Consider the topography and major natural obstacles, like rivers or cliffs, before making your decision.

If a straight-line route is possible, draw it in on your map, place the compass base plate along the line and adjust the rotating bezel until the needle and orienting arrow line up. Keeping these aligned, lift the compass and look along the directional arrow — this will indicate where you want to go.

■ If you want to measure the linear distance between two points on the map, an easy way is to take a piece of paper and align it along the two points, marking their positions on the edge of the paper. Position the paper along the distance scale at the bottom of the map and read off the distance.

If you need to measure a non-linear route, try tracing it with a piece of fine string, then measure the string against the map's distance scale.

A distance roller (also called a map measurer) can be purchased at some specialist outdoor retailers. It enables you to roll a small wheel along the desired route or line, with the actual distance to be covered registered on an easy-to-view dial with multiple scales.

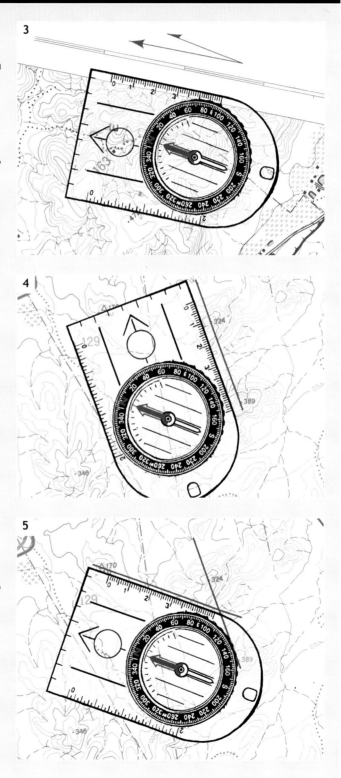

Advances in electronic technology have sparked the arrival of a flood of hi-tech navigational tools onto the outdoor adventure scene.

Global Positioning is a truly groundbreaking development and, as mentioned elsewhere in this chapter, incorporates a triangulation system utilizing a series of orbiting satellites to plot your exact position on earth. Technological advances in cellular telephony have seen many phones incorporating global positioning capability, a feature that makes this powerful navigation tool available to the masses.

GPS TECHNOLOGY HAS MADE NAVIGATION SIMPLER, BUT DON'T RELY ON IT ALONE.

The basic theory

What exactly is a GPS receiver? Originally developed by the US Defence Department as a global navigation system for the military, a number of satellites were launched into orbit in such a way that a sighting may be taken on at least four of them from a specific point on earth at any time.

A 2-D fix (on three satellites) can be used to determine position, while a 3-D fix (on four satellites) enables you to determine altitude as well. Try to lock on to the signal in a relatively open environment, because the high frequencies utilized need a clear line of view and can therefore be blocked by trees, buildings and even your body.

It is very important to have a basic knowledge of orienteering and to have alternative

methods of navigation available as a backup, as electronic gadgets have a tendency to fail. Always make sure you keep a spare set of batteries handy.

Some GPS receivers have an option to download and store electronic maps in their memories, while others simply supply you with the necessary coordinates, enabling you to pinpoint yourself to within about 100m (330ft) on a topographical map. Extra features or additional memory incorporated into the unit may mean an increase in size and weight, so decide which features you need before you buy. Consider the power source; will batteries be available in a remote destination, are they rechargeable and does the unit incorporate a backup power source to protect your data?

Go for rugged, waterproof construction that can handle anything the outdoors throws at it. Make sure you know how to use the unit before you set off.

Practical usage

Being able to accurately pinpoint your location to within a few metres (or feet) brings with it the obvious advantage of always knowing exactly where you are. That is, if you

SATELLITE AND MOBILE TELEPHONES SHOULD BE SAVED FOR EMERGENCIES, NOT USED FOR CASUAL CHATTING.

HIKERS DON'T HAVE THE SPACE TO CARRY LAPTOPS, BUT DOWNLOADING DATA BEFORE SETTING OUT WILL ESTABLISH REFERENCE POINTS FOR MORE CONVENTIONAL NAVIGATION.

have remembered to pack your topographical map. In addition to this, you can use the navigation screen on your GPS as you would an electronic compass (following a bearing or similar). You can also plot way points along a trail by saving coordinates as you progress, thus allowing you to retrace your steps.

Most GPS units will calculate your current speed of advance, extrapolating this information with regard to the distance to your destination, and forecast an estimated time of arrival.

Maps and routes can also be downloaded via the Internet, enabling you to programme a route before you set off. This allows you to correctly identify

possible resupply points beforehand, avoiding the need to carry excess weight along that specific section of the route. And once you're in the field, all you need to do is follow the indications beamed onto the information screen on your receiver. Interfacing the unit with your personal computer at home will allow you to download your route upon your return and print out maps of your journey or save it for future analysis.

The next step

Move beyond the hand-held GPS receiver into the domain of a latter day '007' and you will discover a selection of wearable computers loaded

with an awesome array of features. Arguably leading the field is SUUNTO, offering a chunky, watch-sized instrument incorporating a watch, stopwatch, barometer, altimeter, thermometer, electronic compass and GPS receiver. Satellite phones are a further giant leap for outdoor communications. Using satellite technology similar to that of a GPS, hand sets may be used to co-ordinate emergency supply drops or medical evacuations from the most remote corners of the world. Bionic implants and brain chips cannot be too far off...

WRIST-SIZE COMPUTERS PACK A GREAT DEAL OF INFORMATION INTO A FUNCTIONAL YET WEARABLE FORMAT.

First aid techniques

First aid cannot be learned from a book alone and this section should therefore be seen as informative rather than educational. Before you venture into the wilderness there is no substitute or excuse for not attending a basic first aid course. Many institutions and organizations present up-to-date, affordable and practical courses in most cities and towns.

Ensure that at least two members in the group are sufficiently trained and equipped to treat emergencies and care for an injured person until professional medical assistance arrives. The basic rules of first aid are to preserve life, prevent the medical condition from worsening and promote recovery.

The old adage of prevention being better than cure holds even more true in the wilderness than it does at home. It is therefore essential that individuals with allergies or chronic conditions should inform the group leader. A bee sting allergy might not be a big thing when you are within easy reach of a doctor, but the same situation in a remote wilderness area intensifies the inherent risks. Ensure that your personal first aid kit is adequately stocked with any specific medication you require, and don't rely on the general first aid box.

Basic preventative steps are often easy to implement and may save you a great deal of trouble in the long run. Try in advance to identify any risks you might encounter on your hike and plan preventative strategies, such as carrying enough water to prevent dehydration, wearing a hat and sun block to avoid sunstroke and not taking unnecessary chances. When the chips are down, however, ensure that you are competent and equipped to deal with the situation.

If a medical emergency does arise despite the preventative measures you have taken, remember to stay calm and treat it as soon and as effectively as possible. Thinking clearly and being prepared may be the difference between life and death.

First aid kit

The contents of your medical kit will vary depending on the hiking environment, individual medical conditions and the level of medical expertise within the group.

The following list may serve as a guideline:

BANDAGES, TAPE & PLASTERS: Paper- or adhesive tape, a variety of bandages including crepe, conforming bandages, sterile wound dressings and assorted plasters; triangular slings, sutures, silk strips, sterile gauze swabs, sterile eye pad.

EQUIPMENT: Disposable latex gloves, forceps, scissors, eyebath, thermometer, safety pins, syringes, needles, CPR disposable mouthpiece, splint, thermal blanket.

MEDICATION/OTHER: Burn shield, antiseptic salve, antiseptic liquid, anti-inflammatory gel, paregoric, anti-histamine lotion and tablets, painkillers, electrolyte sachets, saline solution, antifungal ointment.

Preventative measures and treatment of basic conditions

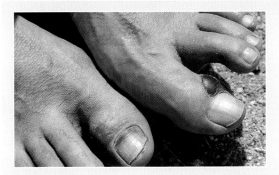

■ TREATMENT: In the case of a sudden pain, treat by applying a cold compress, such as a towel soaked in a mountain stream; if the pain is of a gradual nature, apply heat. Massaging the affected area (to increase blood flow) with a natural remedy like arnica cream or oil may give relief. Use that muscle group sparingly. Try to avoid overdoing things for a while. Rest is advisable if there is no improvement after a few days.

BLISTERS
■ CAUSE: Extreme heat due to constant friction on a particular area of skin.
■ CONDITION: An elevation of the skin filled with serous fluid (or blood in extreme cases).
■ SYMPTOMS: A burning or tender feeling in the affected area.
■ PREVENTION: Make sure boots are well worn-in before setting off on a major hike; avoid hiking with wet socks or shoes as this softens the skin; air your feet whenever you have the opportunity; limit your daily distance; treat a 'hot spot' as soon as irritation sets in by covering with a plaster, adhesive bandage or moleskin.
■ TREATMENT: Avoid breaking the skin and cover the tender area. If the blister grows worse, lance it with a sterilized needle, drain the fluid and apply antiseptic ointment. If an infection sets in, it might be necessary to rest your feet.

MUSCLE STRAINS OR FATIGUE
■ CAUSE: Overexertion of certain muscles.
■ CONDITION: A painful sensation when moving; stiffness in limbs or back due to the presence of micro-tears in the muscle fibres.
■ SYMPTOMS: A sharp (or numb) pain in a specific muscle. Swelling or bruising may occur.
■ PREVENTION: Warm up and stretch before setting out and before lifting a heavy pack.

SUNBURN
■ CAUSE: Overexposure to ultra-violet (UV) radiation from the sun.
■ CONDITION: Reddening and blistering of the skin due to prolonged exposure to the sun.
■ SYMPTOMS: Painfully tender skin with a red and inflamed appearance.
■ PREVENTION: Use high-factor sun block and a lip salve with sun block. Wear a wide-brimmed hat, trousers and a long-sleeved shirt, avoid walking during the middle of the day, and be especially careful at high altitude.
■ TREATMENT: Apply a soothing lotion and stay out of the sun for a few days. Anti-inflammatories such as aspirin or ibuprofen can help to relieve pain. Cool your body by lying in a stream or placing wet towels on affected areas. Severe sun exposure may lead to heatstroke, so check for related symptoms (see below).

HYPERTHERMIA (HEATSTROKE)
■ CAUSE: Continued exposure to sun, excessive temperatures and high humidity, heavy exertion.
■ CONDITION: An abnormal and dangerously high body temperature which may rapidly move beyond heat exhaustion and intensify into heatstroke.
■ SYMPTOMS: A rapid but full pulse, weakening during later stages, a temperature rising beyond 40°C (104°F), ragged breathing, flushed, hot and

Preventative measures and treatment of basic conditions (continued)

dry skin. Hyperthermia can be accompanied by headaches, tiredness, nausea, delirium or confusion, restlessness and convulsions.

■ PREVENTION: Ensure a constant intake of fluids; lower your core temperature by sticking to the shade and walking during the cooler parts of the day; dress lightly, using a base layer to wick moisture away from your skin.

■ TREATMENT: Lowering the body temperature is imperative. Move the casualty to a cool place, remove outer clothing and cover with a wet towel or sheet. Sponge down with water or immerse in a stream until the temperature drops.

Heatstroke is a true emergency as it can be life-threatening. Monitor the casualty constantly as medical attention might be required.

Note: Hyponatremia, a related condition, affects those who over-compensate and drink too much water out of fear of dehydration, thus depleting the body's mineral levels. Slurred speech, nausea, cramps and confusion may occur. Counter with an increased intake of electrolytes and salt.

HYPOTHERMIA (EXPOSURE)

■ CAUSE: Body losing more heat than it produces due to exposure to low temperatures and wind chill.

■ CONDITION: Subnormal body temperatures (more than two degrees below 37°C/98.6°F).

■ SYMPTOMS: The pulse gets weaker and becomes irregular as the level of hypothermia increases, and breathing slows and becomes shallow. Other symptoms are violent shivers; dilated pupils; blueish skin tone and confused, irrational behaviour.

■ PREVENTION: Invest in effective clothing and an appropriate shelter; keep a dry change of clothing on hand; avoid wind chill by finding shelter; take in hot drinks (but not alcohol or caffeine) or food; try to remain active.

■ TREATMENT: Counter and prevent further heat loss (especially through the head and upper body) by dressing the casualty in suitable clothing and wrapping them in a windproof space blanket; remove wet clothing and move to a sheltered, warm environment. Constantly monitor condition.

DIARRHOEA

■ CAUSE: Intake of bacteria and/or viruses into the digestive system.

■ CONDITION: Frequent loose bowel movements.

■ SYMPTOMS: Stomach cramps, with possibly a mild fever and some nausea.

■ PREVENTION: Wash or peel any food that may be contaminated; drink bottled water or purify any water you are unsure of; maintain an acceptable level of personal and camp hygiene.

■ TREATMENT: Avoid spicy or rich foods; take a paregoric or similar medication to counter the symptoms, or allow them to abate naturally.

If chronic diarrhoea, rapid or acute dehydration, weight loss, fatigue or bloody stools set in, consult a medical professional as soon as possible.

Note: Infections such as giardiasis (caused by the *Giardia lamblia* parasite), dysentery (amoebic parasite) and cholera (*Vibrio comma* bacterium), may initially cause symptoms similar to diarrhoea.

DEHYDRATION

- CAUSE: Insufficient intake of fluids; physical exertion or extremely high temperatures. Diarrhoea and vomiting are other contributing factors.
- CONDITION: An acute depletion of bodily fluids.
- SYMPTOMS: Dry mouth, dizziness and headache; similar symptoms to heat exhaustion.
- PREVENTION: Ensure a constant fluid intake; where possible, stick to the shade and walk only during the cooler parts of the day; dress lightly, using a base layer to assist your skin in regulating your core body temperature.
- TREATMENT: Rehydrate the casualty, using a solution high in electrolytic content.

ALTITUDE SICKNESS (also called Acute Mountain Sickness or High-altitude Sickness)

- CAUSE: Ascending rapidly to a high altitude (usually above 3000m/10,000ft).
- CONDITION: A potentially fatal condition, possibly resulting in a build-up of fluid in the lungs (pulmonary oedema) or brain (cerebral oedema).
- SYMPTOMS: Various and diverse. Cerebral oedema often starts with a headache and fatigue, but may progress to include nausea or vomiting, disorientation, rapid heartbeat, a blueish skin tone and eventually unconsciousness, coma or death. Shortness of breath is a key indicator of pulmonary oedema, but other symptoms may also be present.
- PREVENTION: Ascend with caution if you have any of the symptoms mentioned above and descend if they worsen at a given altitude. Acclimatize yourself at various altitude levels, take it easy and do not overexert yourself. Increase your water intake and reduce salt, caffeine and alcohol.
- TREATMENT: Descend immediately to a lower altitude if pronounced symptoms occur; the prescription drug Diamox (acetazolamide) may counter symptoms.

INSECT BITES & STINGS

- CAUSE: Close encounters with creepy crawlies.
- CONDITION: General itching or swelling, broken skin showing bite marks, welts or discolouration.
- SYMPTOMS: Headache, fever, cramps, breathing difficulties, vomiting. Depending on the individual's reaction to the venom, symptoms could range from mild to severe in the case of an acute allergy.
- PREVENTION: To avoid being bitten, apply insect repellent to your body and clothing, keep your tent closed, check your boots, and be aware of the environment and its inhabitants. Take oral antihistamine tablets to help prevent itchiness.
- TREATMENT: Varies according to the cause.
Stings and bites: carefully scrape out stings or wash the bite area with soapy water; soothe with cold compresses or ice. Use antihistamine cream or lotion on unbroken skin around bites or stings to reduce itchiness.
Ticks: dislodge gently with tweezers or heat and disinfect bite area; monitor for signs of infection and tickbite fever symptoms (acute headaches, fever and black colouring around the bite mark).
Leeches: dislodge by applying salt or heat (from a lighted cigarette), clean the area and monitor for signs of infection.

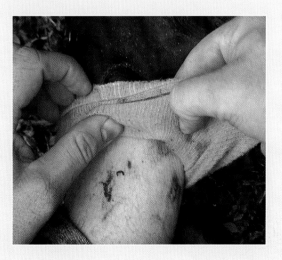

Great global destinations

One of the many attractions of hiking is that you have a whole planet of possible walking destinations waiting to be explored. Soon, your journeys of discovery will take you beyond the borders of your home country, in hot pursuit of dreams of new horizons, strange cultures and exotic locations. While tramping through these faraway destinations, you will find that the slower pace of life and the close personal contact associated with long-distance walking is unbelievably rewarding.

The hikes described in the following pages have been chosen to cover a wide geographical distribution and varying degrees of difficulty. The destinations that have been selected represent both old favourites and new upstarts and differ in duration, terrain and degree of accessibility. However, they are but the tip of the proverbial iceberg and are offered to whet your appetite and let your wanderlust take its own course.

The routes that follow have been graded. Easy (Grade 1–2) is suitable for beginners, while difficult (3–4) might require technical skills for at least part of the trail. Moderate-plus grades have the added effect of altitude. Grades are only there to guide you and should always be considered in conjunction with your own fitness level and your innate ability to persevere when the odds seem stacked against you.

above THE COTSWOLDS ARE A RANGE OF HILLS IN GLOUCESTERSHIRE, ENGLAND, CHARACTERIZED BY SMALL VILLAGES AND GENTLE ROLLING COUNTRYSIDE.

opposite ATOP 300M (1000FT) HIGH CLIFFS, MACHU PICCHU IS A REMNANT OF THE INCA KINGDOM THAT DOMINATED PERU UNTIL THE SPANISH CONQUEST.

United Kingdom: The Cotswold Way

WHERE: The Cotswolds, Gloucestershire, England.

ENVIRONMENT: A delightful English countryside hike, winding through villages resplendent with the Cotswold's famous stone architecture. Sticking to the western escarpment's undulating bridle ways and back roads, the route traverses a rural landscape of hills and dales. Beech woodland, farming hamlets and Iron Age forts offer enticing rest stops along the way.

ROUTE DESCRIPTION: A leisurely pace should see you doing this designated national trail (166km/103 miles) in around a week, but impatient walkers might decide to up the pace. Start at Chipping Camdon and plan overnight stops at Stanton, Cleeve Hill, Birdlip, King's Stanley, Wotton-under-Edge and Old Sodbury before finishing at the historic city of Bath.

FACILITIES & EQUIPMENT: Camping is possible along the route, but it makes more sense to choose from the excellent accommodation available in local inns or bed and breakfasts (B&Bs). Well-organized walkers need little more than a day-pack and comfortable shoes, but be sure to book overnight accommodation before setting off, particularly during peak holiday season and over long weekends (bank holidays).

CONDITIONS: Plan this for summer (June to August) if you want to avoid getting wet, otherwise revel in the chance to test your rainproof gear. The hike is level with a few gentle ups and downs, but easily attainable if you stick to less than 25km (15 miles) per day.

BEST TIME OF YEAR: Mid-May through to August.

GRADING: Easy (Grade 1–2).

THE COTSWOLDS HILLS AND DALES OFFER A PLEASANT HIKING EXPERIENCE THAT IS WITHIN THE LIMITATIONS OF OLDER OR LESS ACTIVE WALKERS.

Europe: The Pilgrim Route to Santiago de Compostela

WHERE: Continental Europe, ending at Santiago de Compostela, a city in Galicia, northwestern Spain.

ENVIRONMENT: Christian pilgrims began the tradition of walking to Santiago de Compostela as early as the 10th century. Today the pilgrimage to this shrine, built over the grave of Saint James the Great (Sant Iago), patron saint of Spain, is made by walkers from all over the world, following a combination of footpaths, high mountain passes and country lanes from as far away as France and Portugal.

ROUTE: A mix of wilderness landscape and ancient history is captured in the many routes that lead into the Galicia region of Spain. Rugged mountains surround tiny *pueblos* (villages), orchards and vineyards, while a multitude of castles and religious shrines line the route to your destination, the breathtakingly beautiful 11th-century cathedral in Santiago.

FACILITIES & EQUIPMENT: Unlike the other hikes covered in this chapter, the majority of walkers who undertake the pilgrimage to Santiago de Compostela do so for spiritual reasons. Hiking routes, which meander through the Pyrenees, past Pamplona and onto Spain's huge inland *mesa* (plain), pass a vast selection of accommodation options, covering everything from rural guesthouses and B&Bs to small hotels. Many religious orders run hospices and overnight shelters. Details are available in most guidebooks or websites covering the route, making it easy to plan your daily pace between these so-called *hospitales* and *refugios*. It is quite feasible to do the route to Santiago de Compostela using a day pack only. Sturdy walking shoes and good socks, a hiking pole, water bottle, and a range of clothing suitable for the wide temperature variations, will suffice.

THE MAGNIFICENT CATHEDRAL AT SANTIAGO DE COMPOSTELA DRAWS CROWDS FROM ALL OVER, MANY OF WHOM ARRIVE ON FOOT, IN THE TIME-HONOURED WAY.

CONDITIONS: As far as European weather goes, you can expect warm to hot days during the summer, although an ascent into the higher mountainous areas will bring with it cooler temperatures. Winters are mild to freezing, again depending on altitude.

BEST TIME OF YEAR: End of March through to August.

GRADING: Easy to moderate (Grade 2).

USA: The John Muir Trail

WHERE: Yosemite and other national parks, California.

ENVIRONMENT: Passing through some of the USA's premier national parks, the JMT traverses spectacular wilderness areas resplendent with grandiose canyons, pristine forests, mountain lakes and a host of sun-kissed peaks towering above 4000m (13,000ft). This is 100 per cent pure wilderness where face-to-face encounters with black bears and mountain lion (cougar or puma) are routine occurrences.

ROUTE DESCRIPTION: Most hikers walk from north to south in order to avoid the huge altitude gains at the southern end of the trail. Kick off in Yosemite National Park and follow the Sierra Nevada for 338km (210 miles) to the southern trailhead at Whitney Portal. Along the way you will pass through King's Canyon and Sequoia national parks and crest the summit of Mount Whitney. Depending on your level of fitness, allow in the region of two to three weeks to complete the entire John Muir Trail. If you have less time, the trail can be done in sections, some as short as a day.

FACILITIES & EQUIPMENT: There are four resupply points along the full route (Tuolumne Meadows, Red's Meadow, Vermillion Valley Resort and Muir Trail Ranch), so some logistical preplanning is possible. A wilderness permit is required and secure barrel canisters must be used to keep provisions safe from bears.

CONDITIONS: Due to the altitude, snow may be encountered in the high reaches well into the summer, while snowfalls start again as early as late October. Terrain along the route varies from lowland meadows to forested river valleys. Steep ascents to high-altitude passes provide some gruelling stretches of hiking.

BEST TIME OF YEAR: Generally July to September.

GRADING: Moderate-plus (Grade 3).

YOSEMITE FALLS, WHICH CASCADES 762M (2500FT) IN THREE LEAPS, IS ONE OF THE MANY SPECTACULAR SIGHTS ALONG THE JOHN MUIR TRAIL, WHICH TRAVERSES THREE NATIONAL PARKS.

New Zealand: Tongariro Northern Circuit

WHERE: Whakapapa village, North Island, New Zealand.

ENVIRONMENT: A stunning tramp into the heartland of three sacred volcanoes, the extinct Tongariro (1967m/ 6455ft), and Ruapehu (2797m/9177ft) and Ngauruhoe (2287m/7504ft), both of which are active. The trail passes through a legendary national park with dual world heritage status and the area is rated by many as New Zealand's premier hiking destination. Volcanic craters and lakes, glacial valleys, boiling mud pools, indigenous woods and tussock grassland make this a varied and spectacular alpine hike not too be missed.

ROUTE DESCRIPTION: The 41km (25 mile) route can be done in anything between four days and a week, but various other options, including day trips to specific huts or areas, may be arranged. A general route plan could take you from the village at Whakapapa to Mangatepopo hut (day one); then to Ketetahi hut (day two); on to New Waihohonu hut (day three) and back to Whakapapa on day four.

FACILITIES & EQUIPMENT: Overnight huts are equipped with mattresses, stoves, drinking water and ablution facilities, but are only serviced during the summer season. Camping is only allowed in designated areas. A pair of stout walking boots is a must.

CONDITIONS: A challenging route through unpredictable terrain, in close proximity to active volcanoes and with the possibility of avalanches during heavy snow falls. Winter conditions change this to a full alpine trip requiring crampons, ice axes and the relevant technical mountaineering equipment. Beware of falling rocks (dislodged by other hikers) and loose scree when attempting an ascent of Tongariro.

BEST TIME OF YEAR: December to March.

GRADING: Difficult (Grade 3—4).

MINERALS IN THE WATER GIVE EMERALD LAKE ITS NAME; AT 1800M (5900FT), RED CRATER (RIGHT) IS THE HIGHEST POINT ON THIS HIKE.

Australia: Blue Mountains National Park Hike

WHERE: The Blue Mountains region near Sydney, New South Wales, Australia.

ENVIRONMENT: Blanketed in eucalyptus forests as far as the eyes can see, the Great Dividing Ranges along Australia's eastern escarpment are popular and accessible hiking destinations for visitors to Sydney. Named for the blue haze rising above millions of gum-trees, the Blue Mountains National Park offers a range of day walks and hikes of varying distance and degrees of difficulty. Hikers delight in exploring the sandstone plateau, which has been battered for innumerable centuries by raging rivers and gusting winds, situated in a gnarled landscape brimming with plunging ravines, heart-stopping cliffs and towering peaks.

ROUTE DESCRIPTION: Despite this being an extremely popular weekend destination, various bush walks, from towns like Katoomba and Blackheath, allow hikers to escape into the solitude of Australia's fourth largest national park. Explore magnificent panoramas on a strenuous two-day hike to Mount Solitary or opt for a selection of day walks through dreamtime scenery filled with trees dating back to the dawn of history.

FACILITIES: The many villages and towns dotting the Blue Mountains region afford visitors a variety of accommodation options, ranging from camping and backpackers' hostels to more upmarket B&Bs, guest houses and hotels. The Blue Mountains Information Centre in Glenbrook, as well as information bureaux in other villages, stock maps and brochures crammed with tourist information. Public transport, by train and taxi, is affordable, while local shops, hostels and adventure operators will be able to cater to most of your immediate needs.

EQUIPMENT: Although some of the day walks are rated as strenuous, moderately fit hikers will be able to complete most of the routes without difficulty. Water bottles or a small day-pack with a hydration bladder are essential. Pack a broad-brimmed hat, a windproof jacket, high-factor sun block and lip salve, insect repellent and some snacks, and ensure your footwear is up to the inhospitable terrain. Book canyoning trips or longer hikes through local adventure operators, enquiring as to the equipment necessary.

CONDITIONS: Care should be taken when outdoors in Australia due to its proximity to the hole in the ozone layer, so remember to 'slip, slop, slap' (local parley for slipping on a shirt, slopping on sun block and slapping on a hat). Average summer temperatures in the Blue Mountains are around 25–29°C (77–85°F), but it cools down from May to September. Highest rainfall occurs between January and July.

BEST TIME OF YEAR: Avoid the school breaks in order to miss the holiday rush.

GRADING: Moderate (Grade 2).

A WIDE RANGE OF TERRAINS, FROM CRAGS AND CLIFFS TO EUCALYPTUS FORESTS, MAKE THE BLUE MOUNTAINS POPULAR WITH LOCALS WHO HIKE THERE REGULARLY.

Southeast Asia: Mount Kinabalu Summit Hike

WHERE: Kinabalu National Park, Sabah region of Borneo, Malaysia.

ENVIRONMENT: Situated to the south of the typhoon belt, Mount Kinabalu (4101m/13,455ft) is Southeast Asia's highest mountain. The terrain surrounding the imposing flat-topped granite peak is breathtakingly diverse, incorporating rice paddies spread in amongst rhododendrons, pitcher plants and montane rainforest. Possible wildlife sightings in the park include bearded pigs, proboscis monkeys and hornbills.

ROUTE DESCRIPTION: Although the ascent of Kinabalu may seem quite daunting, a well-used trail along the southern ridge makes the summit a moderately easy, two-day return trip for fit hikers. The 8.5km (5-mile) tourist route, which starts from the park headquarters, situated at (1500m/4921ft), may be quite crowded so an early start is advisable. A good alternative is to spend a day exploring the 20km (12-mile) trail section around park headquarters. Start the second day from Timpohon gate (1800m/5906ft) and overnight at Laban Rata (3353m/11,000ft), before ascending to reach the summit for dawn views on day three.

FACILITIES & EQUIPMENT: You can do Kinabalu with basic equipment, but good approach shoes, lightweight breathable clothing and a rainproof shell jacket are advisable. Kinabalu is a relatively easy ascent, but the adjacent peaks all require rock climbing skills.

CONDITIONS: Low cloud around the summit may spoil your view, so an extra day in the park is a good idea. Expect maximum temperatures in the low 30s Celsius (90°F) and high humidity throughout the year.

BEST TIME OF YEAR: February to May is the low rainfall period.

GRADING: Moderate (Grade 2–3).

GREETING THE DAWN FROM THE SUMMIT OF MOUNT KINABALU. DESPITE AN ALTITUDE OF 4101M (13,455FT), THIS IS A MODERATELY EASY TWO-DAY TRIP FOR FIT HIKERS, BUT BAD WEATHER CAN INCREASE THE DIFFICULTY FACTOR.

South America: Inca Trail (El Camino Real del Inca)

WHERE: Chilca village, Andes Mountains, Peru.

ENVIRONMENT: Enjoy the wide sky panorama of snow-capped peaks towering above verdant valleys that stretch away as far as the eye can see. Here turbulent rivers and surging waterfalls plunge through prolific forests where ancient ruins will transport you to the era of the Kingdom of the Sun. Mist-drenched forests and lush terraces full of epiphytic orchids and flitting hummingbirds will captivate you along the way.

ROUTE DESCRIPTION: Hike along the Rio Urubamba to camp at Huayallabamba (day one); continue along Dead Woman's Pass to the camp site at Pacaymayo (day two); stop off at Sayacmarca ruins and hike through the Inca tunnels to the camp at Phuyupatamarca (day three); then tackle the final assault past many imposing ruins and through the Sun Gate to arrive at Machu Picchu around midday (day four). Spend your final day exploring the ancient ruins before returning by train to Cuzco.

FACILITIES & EQUIPMENT: Most operators running hikes on the Inca Trail supply all camping equipment except personal items like sleeping bags and mattresses. Porters will carry the bulk of the gear and a team of cooks will make sure you are well fed. Prepare for unpredictable mountain weather by packing clothing able to cope with climatic extremes. Include high UV-protection sun block and sunglasses in your personal day pack.

CONDITIONS: The average hiking altitude along the trail is around 3000m (9800ft), while some rugged sections along the high traverses will occasionally take you as high as 5000m (16,400ft), so you can expect to experience altitude sickness at times. Fairly high humidity, slippery sections in parts of the trail and the possibility of landslides add to the difficulty of this hike.

BEST TIME OF YEAR: May until the end of October.

GRADING: Moderate (Grade 2—3).

ALL ALONG THE INCA TRAIL, HIKERS CAN MARVEL AT THE BUILDING SKILLS OF THE INCA PEOPLE, WHOSE VAST EMPIRE DOMINATED THE ANDES FROM THE 11TH TO THE 16TH CENTURIES.

Africa: Ruwenzori Mountain Hike

WHERE: Ruwenzori National Park, Kasese, Uganda.

ENVIRONMENT: Also known as the mythical Mountains of the Moon, this legendary circular trail in the Ruwenzori ranges is considered by many to be the toughest of Africa's mountain hikes. Rising to 5109m (16,762ft), Margherita Peak on Mt Stanley (the largest glacial area on the continent), is the third tallest peak in Africa (after Kilimanjaro at 5895m/19,340ft and Mt Kenya at 5199m/17,058ft). With four other peaks reaching altitudes of 4700m (15,420ft), the Ruwenzoris offer a surreal hiking experience through Afro-montane vegetation zones where giant lobelia, groundsel and heather species tower as tall as trees. Look out for chimpanzees (the famous mountain gorillas are to be found elsewhere in Uganda), leopards, Ruwenzori touracos, giant forest hogs and forest elephants on the lower slopes.

ROUTE DESCRIPTION: The standard seven-day round trip includes ascending one of the peaks, but various shorter or specialized options can be arranged with operators. Day one (Nyabitaba hut at 2650m/8695ft) and day two (John Matte hut at 3415m/11,205ft), take you into the giant heather zone, with day three a struggle across Bigo Bog to Bujuku hut. A steep ascent, and the possibility of altitude sickness, follows on day four en route to Elana Hut (4543m/14,905ft). Day five involves an early morning start, roping up for the glacier crossing, then ascending Margherita Peak before descending to the hut on beautiful Kitandara Lake. Labour across Freshfield Pass and down to Guy Yeoman hut on day six, before a final and very steep descent through dense bamboo vegetation past Nyabitaba hut to the waiting vehicles (day seven).

FACILITIES: The use of qualified guides with ice climbing experience is imperative. Before leaving, thoroughly check the credentials of your chosen operator to make sure the trip is fully portaged and inclusive of meals. However, if you plan to ascend any of the glacial peaks above the snow line, your party will have to be self-sufficient and geared up to cope with ice climbing (take your own crampons and ice axes).

UGANDA'S RUGGED RUWENZORI RANGE WAS GIVEN THE NAME *LUNAE MONTES*, MOUNTAINS OF THE MOON, IN AD150 BY THE NOTED EGYPTIAN ASTRONOMER AND GEOGRAPHER CLAUDIUS PTOLEMY.

CONDITIONS: Expect it to be cold, wet and muddy, even during the so-called dry season. Rainproof gear and equipment is a must, while a range of sturdy footwear is needed to cope with mud that can be thigh-high, glacial ice and slippery rock. As altitude is a factor, allow sufficient time for acclimatization.

BEST TIME OF YEAR: Mid-December to end February, mid-June to end August.

GRADING: Difficult (Grade 3–4).

Useful map symbols and information

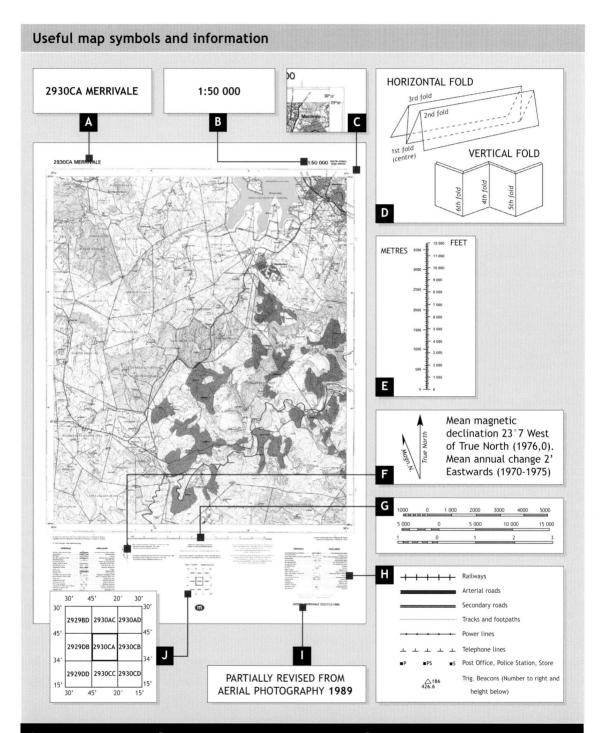

2930CA MERRIVALE

A

1:50 000

B

C

HORIZONTAL FOLD

3rd fold
2nd fold
1st fold (centre)

VERTICAL FOLD

6th fold 4th fold 5th fold

D

METRES 3500 | 12 000 FEET

E

Mean magnetic declination 23°7 West of True North (1976,0). Mean annual change 2' Eastwards (1970-1975)

F

G

H

Railways
Arterial roads
Secondary roads
Tracks and footpaths
Power lines
Telephone lines
■P ■PS ■S Post Office, Police Station, Store
△186
426.6 Trig. Beacons (Number to right and height below)

	30'	45'	20'	30'	
30'					30'
		2929BD	2930AC	2930AD	
45'					45'
		2929DB	2930CA	2930CB	
34°					34°
		2929DD	2930CC	2930CD	
15'					15'
	30'	45'	20'	15'	

J

I

PARTIALLY REVISED FROM AERIAL PHOTOGRAPHY **1989**

A MAP NAME AND UNIQUE NUMBER. **B** SCALE SHOWING THE RATIO IN CM/METRES OR IN/FEET. **C** MINUTES AND DEGREES EAST/WEST AND NORTH/SOUTH. **D** THE CORRECT (AND EASIEST) WAY TO FOLD A LARGE MAP. **E** CONVERSION TABLE FOR METRIC AND IMPERIAL DISTANCES. **F** MAGNETIC DECLINATION (DIFFERENCE IN DEGREES BETWEEN TRUE AND MAGNETIC NORTH). **G** DISTANCE SCALE (M/FT; KM/MILES). **H** LEGEND/KEY TO SYMBOLS USED TO INDICATE NATURAL OR MAN-MADE STRUCTURES. **I** DATE OF PRINTING OR LAST REVISION. **J** THE POSITION OF THIS MAP IN RELATION TO OTHERS IN A SERIES.

Planning check list

MUST HAVES:

☐	Backpack
☐	Sleeping bag and sleeping bag liner
☐	Camping mattress (foam pad or airbed)
☐	Tent, bivy bag or groundsheet
☐	Stove and fuel
☐	Matches (waterproof) or lighter
☐	Cooking pot (mess kit) and cooking utensils
☐	Plate, bowl, mug and eating utensils
☐	Multi-tool or pocket knife
☐	Lantern (butane or candle-power)
☐	Flashlight or head torch
☐	Water bottles or bladder-type hydration systems
☐	Walter filter and/or purification tablets
☐	Sunglasses
☐	First-aid kit and personal medication
☐	Space (emergency) blanket
☐	Insect repellent
☐	Sun screen and lip salve
☐	Personal toiletries and small towel
☐	Toilet paper and folding spade or trowel
☐	Garbage bags or bin liners
☐	Waterproof raincover for your pack
☐	Whistle
☐	Length of rope
☐	Rip-stop tape for general repairs
☐	Permits and paperwork
☐	Entry fees (if required to pay at trailhead)
☐	Topographical maps and/or guidebooks

☐	GPS and/or compass and pencil
☐	Watch
☐	Emergency rations
☐	Food (as determined by the weather and the duration of the hike)
☐	*Clothing:* (Note — layering is the key to comfort.)
☐	• Long pants suitable for expected weather
☐	• Shorts or zip-off long pants
☐	• Tracksuit, leggings or long underwear bottoms
☐	• T-shirts (long and/or short sleeved)
☐	• Warm undershirt for cold conditions
☐	• Outer shirt (cool for summer, warm for winter)
☐	• Fleece or pile windproof jacket
☐	• Waterproof outer layer (pants and hooded jacket)
☐	*Footwear:* boots, approach shoes or sandals
☐	*Socks:* lightweight synthetic liners and heavier wool-blend or synthetic socks
☐	• Gloves and scarf for cold weather
☐	*Headgear:* beanie or woollen balaclava for cold; wide-brimmed hat for sun protection
☐	*Rain gear:* suitable for the expected conditions

OPTIONAL ITEMS:

☐	Camera and memory cards
☐	Hiking poles
☐	Needle and thread for essential repairs
☐	Journal (notebook) and pen
☐	Binoculars
☐	Field guides
☐	Assorted plastic and zip-lock bags

Further reading and useful resources

FLETCHER, COLIN and CHIP RAWLINS. *The Complete Walker*. 4th edition. Knopf, 2002.

LOGUE, VICTORIA. *Backpacking: Essential Skills to Advanced Techniques*. Alabama: Menasha Ridge Press, 2000.

TOWNSEND, CHRIS. *The Backpacker's Handbook*. Ragged Mountain Press, 1996.

GILCHRIST, TOM. *The Trekkers Handbook*. Cicerone Press, 1996.

McMANNERS, HUGH. *101 Essential Tips: Hiking*. London: Dorling Kindersley, 2000.

LOGUE, VICTORIA and FRANK. *The Appalachian Trail Back-packer. Trail-proven Advice for Hikes of any Length*. Alabama: Menasha Ridge Press, 1994.

BRYSON, BILL. *A Walk in the Woods: Rediscovering America on the Appalachian Trail*. Broadway Books, 1999.

HJELLSTROM, BJORN and NEWT HEISLEY. *Be Expert with Map and Compass*. Hungry Minds Inc., 1994.

WINNET, THOMAS and KATHY MOREY. *Guide to the John Muir Trail*. 3rd edition. Wilderness Press, 1998.

REYNOLDS, KEV. *Walks and Climbs in the Pyrenees* (1997); *Walking in the Alps* (1998). Cumbria: Cicerone Press.

SHARP, HILARY. *Trekking and Climbing in the Western Alps*. London: Globetrotter, 2002.

MEAD, ROWLAND. *Walking the Cathedral Cities of Western England*. London: New Holland, 2001. (Other titles in the Walking series include Amsterdam, Paris, Edinburgh, Dublin).

KLINGE, SVEN. *Classic Walks of Australia*. New Holland, 2000.

WILLIAMS, BRUCE and REECE SCANNEL. *The Blue Mountains on Foot*. Sydney: New Holland, 2002.

KLINGE, SVEN and ADRIAN HART. *Don't Die in the Bush*. Sydney: New Holland, 2000; LEARY, P.M. South African edition, Cape Town, 1994.

RAZZETTI, STEVE. *Top Treks of the World*. New Holland, 2001.

OLIVIER, WILLIE and SANDRA. *Exploring the Natural Wonders of South Africa*. Cape Town: Struik, 1999.

PATERSON-JONES, COLIN. *Best Walks of the Garden Route*. Cape Town: Struik, 1998.

HATTINGH, GARTH. *The Outdoor Survival Manual*. New Holland, London, 2000.

WILSON, KEN and RICHARD GILBERT. *Classic Walks* and *The Big Walks*. Diadem.

Walking Magazine staff. *The Walker Within: 45 Stories of Motivation and Inspiration for Walkers*. The Lyons Press, 2001.

Useful resources:
• *Globetrotter Guides and Maps* www.newhollandpublishers.com
• *Walks Worldwide Guides* www.walksworldwide.com
• *Backpacker Magazine* www.bpbasecamp.com
• *Great Outdoor Recreation Pages* www.gorp.com
• *The Great Outdoors Magazine* tgo@calmags.co.uk
• *National Geographic Adventure Magazine* adventure@ngs.org
• *World-wide Fund for Nature* www.panda.org
• *Lonely Planet Walking Guides* www.lonelyplanet.com
• *Outward Bound* www.outwardbound.org
• *Hiking and Walking homepage* www.webwalking.com
• *Canadian National Parks* www.parcscanada.gc.ca
• *The Backpacker website* www.thebackpacker.com
• *Gear reviews* www.gearreview.com

Making contact

Although there is no global controlling body for hiking, most countries have national organizations able to provide information on national trails. Adventure travel companies are another source of information.

WORLDWIDE
KE Adventure Travel
32 Lake Road, Keswick,
Cumbria CA12 5DQ, UK.
Tel: +44 (1768) 773-966
Fax: +44 (1768) 774-693
info@keadventure.co.uk
www.keadventuretravel.com

Walks Worldwide
15 Main Street, High Bentham,
Lancaster LA2 7LG, UK.
Tel: +44 (1524) 262-255
Fax: +44 (1524) 262-229
sales@walksworldwide.com
www.walksworldwide.com

Classic Journeys
33 High Street, Tibshelf,
Alfreton, Derbyshire DE55 5NX.
Tel: +44 (1773) 873-497
www.classicjourneys.co.uk

Sherpa Expeditions
131a Heston Road,
Hounslow TW5 0RF, UK.
Tel: +44 (20) 8577-2717
Fax: +44 (20) 8572-9788
www.sherpa-walking-holidays.co.uk

Explore Worldwide
1 Frederick St, Aldershot,
Hants GU11 1LQ, UK
Tel: +44 (1252) 760-000
Fax: +44 (1252) 760-001
info@exploreworldwide.com
www.exploreworldwide.com

USA
American Hiking Society
1422 Fenwick Lane
Silver Spring, MD 20910.
Tel: +1 (301) 565-6704
www.americanhiking.org

National Park Service (USA)
Director NPS, 1849 C Street NW,
Washington DC 20240.
Tel: +1 (202) 208-6843
www.nps.gov

John Muir Trail: contact Yosemite
Association, a non-profit
organization that assists YNP.
PO Box 545, Yosemite National
Park, California 95389.
Tel: +1 (209) 372-0310/372-0740
info@pcta.org
www.pcta.org/jmt

UK/EUROPE
C-N-Do Walking Holidays
Unit 32, Stirling Enterprise Park,
Stirling FK7 7RP, Scotland.
Tel/fax: +44 (1786) 445-703
info@cndoscotland.com
www.btinternet.com/~cndo.scotland

Exodus Adventure Tours
9 Weir Road,
London SW12 0LT, UK.
Tel: +44 (20) 8675-5550
Fax: +44 (20) 8673-0779
info@exodus.co.uk
www.exodus.co.uk

AUSTRALIA
Hike for Life
PO Box 211, L1 Walkabout Centre
Woy Woy, NSW 2256.
Tel: +61 (02) 4344-1173
www.hikeforlife.com

NEW ZEALAND
Adventure World Travel
101 Great South Road
Remeura, Auckland.
Tel: +64 (9) 524-5118
Fax: +64 (9) 520-6629
discover@adventureworld.com

SOUTH AFRICA
Cape Nature Conservation
Private Bag X9086
Cape Town 8000
Tel: +27 (021) 483-4051
Fax: +27 (021) 423-0939
cncinfo@cape-town.org
www.capenature.org.za

South African National Parks
PO Box 787
Pretoria 0001.
Tel: +27 (012) 428-9111
Fax: +27 (012) 343-0905
Reservations@parks-sa.co.za
www.parks-sa.co.za

DISABLED HIKING
Handi-Cap Evasion
Ch. de la Creuzette, 69270
Fontaines sur Saone, France.
www.hce.assoc.fr/eng

Index

Photographic credits

NHIL/Jacques Marais: pp6-7, 8, 14, 17, 19, 24 (right), 33, 35 (top), 38 (a), 42, 46, 48 (top), 56 (below), 62 (top), 70 (below), 82 (top left); NHIL/Nicholas Aldridge: pp24 (left), 25 (right), 27 (below left & right), 28, 29 (centre), 30, 31 (left & top right), 35 (below), 36 (b, c, e & f), 37 (a, b, c & d), 38 (d), 43, 47, 52, 53, 73 (below), 78, 82 (top); Struik Image Library (SIL)/Shaen Adey: pp40, 68; Andy Belcher: pp15, 54, 61; Dugald Bremner: pp11, 23, 60 (below); Scarre Cilliers: p73 (centre); John Cleare: p80; Alan Copson Pictures: p88; Ingrid Corbett: p90; Leslie Garland Picture Library/Alamy: p13; Paul Glendell: p84; V.K. Guy: p82 (below); Paul Harris: pp41, 48 (below), 65; Bill Hatcher: pp56 (top), 57, 64, 69 (top); Garth Hattingh: p67 (top); Hedgehog House (HH)/Colin Monteath: pp2, 59, 73 (top); (HH)/Pat Barrett: p10; HH/Tony Brunt: p71; Jack Jackson: p45 (top); Katadyn: p38 (e); Johan Kloppers: p18 (below); LOOK/Christian Heeb: p86; LOOK/Holger Leue: p87; LOOK/Karl-Heinz Raach: p85; Fiona Macintosh: p91; Jacques Marais: pp12 (below), 21, 22 (below), 25 (left), 29 (below), 32 (top), 35 (centre), 39, 44, 51, 60 (top), 62 (centre and below), 67 (below), 70 (top), 76 (below), 77 (top), 79, 81; Christelle Marais: pp12 (top left), 18 (top), 29 (top), 30 (left); Petzl/Lyon Equipment: p36 (a); Picture Box/JF Hagenmuller: p66; Pictures Colour Library: pp83, 89; Glenn Randall: pp4-5, 49; Richard Sale: pp20, 66; Travel Ink/Tony Page: p9; Stockshot/E Williams/M Glaister: p63; Stockshot/D Willis: p50.

Publisher's acknowledgements

The publishers wish to thank the following suppliers for their assistance in providing clothing and equipment for photoshoots and/or permission to use existing photographs: Capestorm: www.capestorm.co.za; Cape Union Mart: www.capeunionmart.co.za; First Ascent: www.firstascent.co.za; Garmin: www.garmin.com; Karrimor Ltd: www.karrimor.com; Suunto: www.suunto.com; Thermarest/MSR/Cascade Designs: www.thermarest.com